D0469698

A Peek Behind the Curtain

AT PUBLIC SCHOOLS
& SPECIAL EDUCATION

A Peek Behind the Curtain

AT PUBLIC SCHOOLS & SPECIAL EDUCATION

Daniel Lauretano

Deeds Publishing | Athens

Copyright © 2021 — DANIEL LAURETANO

ALL RIGHTS RESERVED—No part of this book may be reproduced in any form or by any electronic or mechanical means, including information storage and retrieval systems, without permission in writing from the author, except by a reviewer who may quote brief passages in a review.

Published by Deeds Publishing in Athens, GA
www.deedspublishing.com

Printed in The United States of America

Cover design by Mark Babcock.

ISBN 978-1-950794-55-3

Books are available in quantity for promotional or premium use. For information, email info@deedspublishing.com.

First Edition, 2021

10 9 8 7 6 5 4 3 2 1

This book is dedicated to the hard-working teachers, paraeducators, administrators, and school staff who…every single day…go above and beyond to educate, support, protect, and inspire students.

CONTENTS

The secret in education lies in respecting the student.

— *Ralph Waldo Emerson*

INTRODUCTION

It has been my privilege over the years to have had the opportunity to work with hundreds of special education students and their parents. Special ed teachers are afforded a significant advantage … we often get to work with children over the course of many years. A student might qualify for services in kindergarten, for example, and still be eligible for services in 5th grade. We have the opportunity over those years to truly and deeply get to know their unique strengths, challenges, needs, and learning styles. We also get to know their parents for several years … plenty of time to develop an effective working relationship with them as they and their child navigate their way through the grades.

Several of the stories in this collection share a theme … teachers helping to facilitate effective parental involvement in their child's educational journey. I learned, early in my career, that parents are an integral cornerstone of the teamwork that must be in place to ensure ongoing successes by their sons and daughters in special education … children who carry with them an extra burden of inherent or acquired challenges that have created frustrations and failures along the way.

Parents might need help in bolstering their child's self-concept and/ or motivation, or assistance in learning specific academic processes and strategies so they can effectively augment what is being taught at school. Certainly, parents and teachers must establish and share individually tailored goals and realistically-high expectations, which is only accomplished through clear, ongoing communication and positive teamwork.

There are other stories that recount some challenging experiences and interactions I experienced at school, and the behind-the-scenes realities of those situations. Now, I understand that the title of this book might conjure up thoughts of me sharing deficiencies and 'dirty little secrets' of places I've worked...but nothing could be further from the truth. During my career as a special education teacher, I had the privilege and good fortune to work in schools and districts that are extremely progressive, ultra-professional, and undisputed leaders in the field of education in the state of Washington. But even working under such optimal conditions, I wasn't shielded from experiencing several intense challenges and harrowing situations.

On the other hand, there are a couple of stories that I wrote just for fun. They color a bit outside the lines...there are no suggested teaching strategies or relevant revelations in these. You'll know them when you read them.

I'd like to extend my heartfelt appreciation to all those who work in schools and school districts who have had to endure the extraordinary challenges brought on by the pandemic. The same sentiments go out to all students and parents. They all deserve our deepest gratitude and respect for the exceptional efforts they've put forth during these difficult times.

I'd also like to take a moment to give a shout-out to an indispensable group of individuals...paraeducators (or 'paraprofessionals' as they're called in some districts). Because of the nature of their positions, their hard work is sometimes under-appreciated and overlooked. My good fortune over the years as an educator certainly included working with amazing, dedicated paraeducators; I have the ultimate respect for, and appreciation of, all they do 'behind the scenes' in our schools.

TWO BIRDS ON A WIRE

Several kids walked into the Resource Room about a minute into the afternoon recess.

"Mr. H, is it okay if we spend our recess in here today?" asked Easton, the first kid in the door.

"It's totally okay with me," Mr. H replied. "But it's a beautiful day out there, a great chance to enjoy some sunshine. We don't get that chance very often in Tacoma in March."

"I don't care about the sun," said Rebecca. "I like it in here."

"I'm happy to hear that," he said. "It's great to see you all ... welcome!"

Mr. H smiled as he went back to his paperwork. He thought it was great that non-special education students were so happy and willing to come in and hang out in the Resource Room every now and then. He and his special ed team had worked hard to create that welcoming, all-inclusive climate in their room. He could remember past years when the stigma of *the special ed room* made general education students wary of crossing the threshold. To him, times like today were one more indication special ed students were no longer seen as outcasts.

"Yes, you are always welcome to come hang out in our room," he thought to himself.

His paraeducator, Mrs. Dwyer, was busily prepping for her reading group, which would begin right after recess. She looked up from her stacks of books and said, "You know, my next group of 2nd graders is probably going to finish up level one of Reading Mastery by the end of the week. That'll mean your morning group and my group will be having to share the text books for level two."

"Thanks for the heads-up," Mr. H said. "Tell you what...when we finish our group each morning, I'll leave the books and the Teacher's Guide on your shelf. And then when I come in each morning, I'll grab them back."

"We have a plan then," smiled Mrs. Dwyer. "Oh, by the way, I saw Maria's mom at the grocery store over the weekend. She said to say hello. Maria's been doing much better over at Fordham the past couple of months."

It had been a tough first half of the year for Maria in middle school, so that was nice news for Mr. H to hear. "That's great to hear," he said. "I miss her... glad she's doing okay. Hope she comes to visit sometime."

After several minutes of work, he glanced over at the clock. "Okay everyone, one minute until the bell. Please close out of your games, or put away your art supplies. Oh, and Marco, please don't shut the tablet off when you close your game. And there's the bell...great to have you here today... have a great rest of the day!"

"Bye, everyone...have a great afternoon!" Mrs. Dwyer called to them. She was one of those people who loved every student, and they loved her right back. Mr. H knew how lucky he was to have her as a partner.

The 2nd grade reading group and the 4th grade math group started trickling in. "Hi Mrs. Dwyer! Hi Mr. H!" said Nasir, as he walked in smiling. He took a seat at Mrs. Dwyer's table. Several students followed, three more joining Nasir, and five settling in at Mr. H's table after taking a quick post-recess drink of water.

"Hi everyone," said Mr. H. "I hope you had a great recess; let's settle in and get right to work. But first, a quick review of what we learned yest..."

The intercom interrupted, "Excuse me, Mr. H?" It was Mrs. Copeland, the Office Manager.

"Yes, Mrs. Copeland?"

"I am so sorry to interrupt your group. Would you be available to respond to an issue out on the playground? I have no one else to ask at the moment."

"Yes, I could do that."

"Thank you, Mr. H. You'll find Mrs. Nicholson with a student in the big toy area."

"I'm on my way. Let her know I'll be there in about two minutes."

"I will. Thank you."

"Okay folks, sorry this is happening again. But it's important to be flexible in life, right, because sometimes things come up that we weren't expecting. So, change of plans... um, okay. We only got about two-thirds of the way through yesterday's workbook pages, so let's open up to page 83 please, we'll start with that today. You can finish that up while I'm gone. Mrs. Dwyer will be in the room with you, so if you have any questions, please ask her.

"Mrs. Dwyer, excuse me, they should all be able to work independently on this workbook assignment, so there should be no reason for talking... or for not working," he said as he glanced around the table, briefly catching the eyes of each student.

"I'll keep an eye on them, Mr. H," she replied. "These kids are all very responsible, I'm sure they'll do fine."

"Thank you," he said as he walked from the table over to the door. "I'll be back as soon as I can." He and Mrs. Dwyer had been through this many times over the years. When Mr. H was called away to respond to situations, they knew he might be back in five minutes, or in an hour or more. Every situation was different.

The Resource Room was in a portable building right at the edge of the playground, so he could already see the situation at the big toy area as he walked down the ramp from the portable. A 1st grade boy named Sam, who was one of his special education students, was sitting cross-legged in the pea gravel under the slide of the big toy. Mrs. Nicholson was standing near him.

"Hi, Mrs. Nicholson... hi Sam," he said as he approached them. "What seems to be the problem here?"

"Well, Sam refuses to go in from recess," said Mrs. Nicholson. "When the bell rang and everyone lined up, we noticed that Sam was still playing by himself out at the far edge of the playfield. When I walked out there to ask him to come line up, he ran from me, over here to the big toy and sat down under the slide. He's refusing to talk to me, or to follow my directions to go to his classroom."

"Okay, thank you. I know you have a kindergarten group that's waiting on you, Mrs. Nicholson. So, tell you what, I've got this... you can go ahead and go inside."

"Thank you, Mr. H."

"You're welcome. Thank you for helping Sam, and have a great afternoon."

As Mrs. Nicholson left the area, Mr. H walked over and scooched down in the pea gravel a few feet in front of Sam. "Alright buddy, I'm going to help you with this...but since I don't know what happened, I need you to talk with me and tell me what's going on."

Sam looked at him through teared-up eyes. "I was playing out on the field. I didn't know recess was over, and Mrs. Nickerson walked out and told me it was time to go line up. But everyone that was lined up, they were all looking at me, and I felt like a dumb head. So, I ran over here to hide."

Mr. H pictured the situation as it had probably unfolded. Sam was a student with significant attention deficits, which was one of the reasons he was a special ed student. His team worked with many students with ADHD (Attention-Deficit/Hyperactivity Disorder), but Sam was by far the most impacted. Do you know the humorous anecdote where a kid would be listening one moment and then go 'Oh, squirrel!' and lose focus? Well, Sam wouldn't be listening at the beginning of that anecdote, and he wouldn't even notice the squirrel. He was that tuned out from what was going on around him. So, Mr. H surmised that because Sam had been out at the far edge of the field, he probably hadn't noticed the bell when it rang. And because of his location, he also had no students rushing past him to go line up, which would have been the usual cue to Sam that recess was over.

"Okay buddy, first of all, you're not in trouble. I know you're a little upset, and it's hard for *anybody* to talk with people when they're upset, so thank you for talking with me. Let me just make sure I understand... you didn't know recess was over, and that's why you didn't line up. Is that right?"

Sam shook his head 'yes'.

"I'd like you to use your words, please."

"Yes, I didn't know."

"I totally believe you. Now, I'd like to talk for a minute about what you could and should have done better here. When Mrs. Nicholson asked you to go line up, she was giving you directions. And after a few minutes, after all of the lines had gone into the building and no other students were watching you, there was no reason to keep sitting here. I know you were upset, and that made it harder to follow her directions. Is that right?"

"Yes."

"I understand. But Sam, it's important to follow directions even when you're angry or upset... which I know isn't the easiest thing in the world to do. But I know you'll be able to learn to do that. Tell you what... I'm going to walk with you to your classroom. You are *not* in trouble. We have our social skills group a little later, and in today's group we're going to talk about being able to make good choices even when something goes a little bit wrong. Kind of like what happened here. These kinds of things happen in life, and it's important to be able to get past them and still have a great day. And I know that you can have an awesome rest of the day. Sound good?"

"Sounds good," Sam said, drying his eyes and then wiping his nose with the sleeve of his coat.

After walking Sam to his classroom, Mr. H walked quickly back to the Resource Room. He paused in front of Mrs. Dwyer's table, and waited for Candice to finish the sentence she was reading. Mrs. Dwyer said, "Excuse me for a second, everyone. Mr. H, your students have been working hard while you were gone, no talking... working hard the whole time!"

"Awesome, you guys! I'm proud of you. Thank you, Mrs. Dwyer. And great job reading, Candice!"

Back at his table, he said, "Sorry I had to leave for a while, but terrific job of working hard while I was gone. Totally awesome! Okay, close your workbooks please, and let's get to today's lesson." Toward the end of their session, he decided to give them a few minutes of reward fun time for being so responsible.

The rest of the day went well for Sam. During his social skills group that afternoon with Dean and Sydney, Sam relatively-enthusiastically listened and participated in the lesson. The main topic was learning and using strategies to recover from bad decisions, or from things not going as planned. Mr. H talked about how important that skill is both at school and at home, and even had the kids do some role-playing to practice the strategies. The role-play scenario walked them through some specific strategy steps... taking a deep breath, counting slowly to five, and then saying something positive, like 'I got this!'. It would take time, but he was confident they would make significant progress in this important area.

They had an advantage a lot of kids don't get... they were learning social skills and strategies at a very young age.

After school, he swung by Sam's classroom to speak with his teacher. They brainstormed some ideas, and decided to choose two or three responsible classmates who could keep an eye out for Sam toward the end of recess times, and discreetly prompt him to line up if he needed such a prompt. He also emailed the same request to the paraeducators who supervised recesses. And he put a reminder on his calendar to talk with Sam the next morning. He wanted to ask him to avoid playing at the far edge of the play field, and to play with other kids instead of by himself. After all, it's much more fun to play with friends at recess.

On his drive home, he kept thinking about Sam...it was great he'd been able to finish the day on a positive note. Sam had carved out a special place in his heart, and Mr. H felt good about how much he had progressed since the beginning of the school year. As he got to his exit ramp off the highway, he took a deep breath and said out loud, "Okay, this is where I leave my day behind me... no more thinking about work! I got this!"

He stopped at the end of a short line of cars in the left turn lane. He looked out his window at the snow-covered foothills in the distance, then turned his gaze upward to a long line of birds all perched along the power lines. There must have been thirty or so birds, all just hanging out together. He wasn't sure what caused it, but suddenly all of the birds took off in different directions at the same time... except one bird, who remained on the wire all by himself. Mr. H chuckled to himself, "See, now that would be Sam, not tuned in to his surroundings, not even noticing when everyone around him flew off in a total frenzy! Yeah, that would totally be Sam if he was a bird." He returned his gaze to the lane in front of him... the light was turning from yellow to red, and the three or four cars that had been in front of him were gone.

LITTLE BLUE DOLPHINS

I couldn't for the life of me understand how things had spun so totally out of control. There I was, minding my own business, when I got completely blindsided. How I got mixed up in the situation in the first place was a mystery to me…until it wasn't.

I was in my classroom one day after school, about a half-hour after the students had gone home. My principal, Mrs. Carrier, called and asked me to swing by her office before I went home that day. I told her I would…that I could come right away. I had a meeting to get to at the Special Services building, but I had enough time to swing by.

When I walked into her office, she asked me to shut the door. This was fairly common; as the school's special education teacher, I was often involved in confidential conversations about students. But I was about to find out that this was not going to be anything resembling a common conversation.

"I have something kind of unusual to speak with you about," Mrs. Carrier said. "I just got a call from Nora Ford's mother…she wanted to know why you gave Nora a pair of earrings. She said that when Nora got home today, she unpacked Nora's backpack and found a pair of dolphin-shaped earrings in there. When she asked Nora where she got them, Nora told her you gave them to her. Mrs. Ford is really upset, and wants to know what's going on. So first, sorry, but I have to ask...did you give Nora earrings?"

"No, I didn't," I replied. "I would never give a gift like that to a student."

"I was sure you didn't, and I told Mrs. Ford that I was sure you didn't. Would you please give her a call to let her know?"

"I'll be happy to do that," I said. "I have a meeting to go to, but I'll call her as soon as I get out. As you know, she and I go back several years...I had her older daughter Kelsie as a special ed student a few years back...she knows me and trusts me. I just wonder why Nora said I gave those to her."

"Me too. Thanks for following up on this. Tomorrow, let me know how the conversation goes."

"I will. Have a good night."

"You too."

After I got out of my meeting, I gave Mrs. Ford a call.

"Hello, Mrs. Ford...this is Mr. L. Mrs. Carrier asked me to give you a call. How can I help you?"

"Hi Mr. L...thanks for calling. Nora's telling me you gave her this pair of earrings she came home with today. I'm just wondering if that's true?"

"It's totally *not* true. I have no idea why she's saying that, but she didn't get them from me."

"That's what I figured. Hang on a second. Nora...come in here. Mr. L's on the phone, and he says he didn't give those earrings to you."

There was a pause for several seconds, then Mr. L could hear Nora say, "Yes he did. He gave them to me today when I was in the Resource Room. It was this afternoon in our reading group when I was there with Dierdre."

"She said she got them from you this afternoon when she was in the Resource Room with Dierdre."

I was shocked to hear that. "Nora was in my room with Dierdre this afternoon, but I certainly didn't give her any earrings. We had our normal group, and then they both left together. Wow. Can you tell her that I guess we'll have to have a meeting here at the school, hopefully tomorrow, with Mrs. Carrier and you Mrs. Ford, and Nora, and her classroom teacher Mrs. Anders and me…so we can talk about this as a group? Hopefully, she'll hear that and change her mind about sticking with that story."

I heard Mrs. Ford tell her about the potential meeting.

"Okay, we can have a meeting tomorrow," Nora said. "Do I get to keep the earrings?"

"Well, she's not changing her story," said Mrs. Ford. "Looks like we should go ahead and schedule that meeting so we can get to the bottom of this."

"Okay, I'll talk with Mrs. Carrier first thing tomorrow morning. She'll call you to schedule the meeting. I'm sure that when Nora sees all the people in Mrs. Carrier's office, she'll tell us the truth."

"Okay, thank you for calling, Mr. L. I'll wait to hear from Mrs. Carrier then. See you soon."

"See you soon. Have a good night."

"Thank you, you too."

I was fairly bewildered. Why on earth was Nora telling her mom that lie? Although it wasn't true, I didn't like the possibility that people might start talking about it. Interestingly, my last name is very similar to the last name of an infamous teacher from the Puget Sound region who spent prison time for a highly publicized affair she'd had with a young boy. During the months of the news story, I had been asked more than once if I was related to the woman who was in jail. Each time, I would smile and address the similar but different pronunciations of our last names.

But this was different; this was my real name being potentially questioned and smeared. It helped that I was certain Nora wouldn't be able to look a roomful of adults in the eye and continue with this lie at the upcoming meeting.

The next morning, I swung by the office to speak with Mrs. Carrier. After telling her about the conversation with Mrs. Ford, I thanked her in advance for any help she could give me in resolving the uncomfortable situation as soon as possible. She promised to schedule the meeting as soon as it worked for everyone's schedules.

The meeting turned out being arranged for after school that same day. It would be in Mrs. Carrier's office, with Mrs. Carrier, Mrs. Ford, Nora, Mrs. Anders, and me. I looked forward to getting the whole matter over with.

When Mrs. Ford arrived, everyone was already sitting in Mrs. Carrier's office, including Nora. After all of the greetings, the group got right down to business.

"So, Nora," said Mrs. Carrier, "we would all like to hear what you have to say about those earrings you brought home yesterday. Can you tell us where you got them, please?"

Nora looked right at Mrs. Carrier and said, "Mr. L gave them to me, yesterday during my reading group in the Resource Room."

Mrs. Carrier replied, "I'd like you to look right at Mr. L please, and tell that to him."

"You gave them to me yesterday in the Resource Room. When I was in there with Dierdre."

"Now Nora, you know that isn't true," I said. "Why would you make up a story like that?"

"I'm not making it up...you gave them to me."

Mrs. Carrier jumped back in, "Nora, I spoke with Dierdre today, and she said she didn't see Mr. L give them to you."

"He gave them to me when she wasn't looking."

For whatever reason, Nora was sticking to that story. She and I had a terrific relationship…we had worked together for two years at that point, and there had never been any turbulence or reasons for her to be mad at me or to 'get even' with me about anything. Why was she trying to get me in trouble? I had been sure she'd change her tune in front of an office full of adults. I had been wrong. And now I was starting to get a little worried. Rumors are a nasty thing to have floating around out there, especially when they're about a male teacher grooming and gifting a young girl. A vulnerable, cute young special ed girl he has direct influence over.

The meeting finished up without anything getting resolved. So now it looked like a classic 'your word versus mine' kind of situation. My reputation was impeccable, and I wanted to keep it that way. Frankly, I didn't know what to do. I don't think anyone did.

What would the next step be? If I was Nora's parent, I'd be livid if I knew for sure my daughter was receiving jewelry from a male teacher. That action would raise all sorts of red flags. So, what could I expect from Mrs. and Mr. Ford?

I started going over my own list of possible things to do. Should I confront Nora, and demand that she tell the truth? No, that might look to others like I was trying to influence her, or badger her. What were Mrs. Carrier's options, and what were Mr. and Mrs. Ford's options? To tell you the truth, I was a combination of scared, confused, and angry that night, hating the possibility that the reputation I'd worked so hard to build was in jeopardy. I didn't sleep too well, wondering what the next day would bring.

Before school the next morning, I sat in the Resource Room, speaking with my paraeducator and friend, Mrs. Skyler. She worked with Nora every day, like I did, and was just as surprised as I was that Nora would be lying about something that could potentially do significant damage to my career. She said that she wished she could help in some way. I told her I wished she could, too.

I got a call from Mrs. Carrier, asking if I was free to come up to her office. I told her I'd be right there.

"I wish this wasn't coming to this," she said, "but now Mr. and Mrs. Ford want to arrange another meeting... this time, without Nora. I'm sorry to say...they've called the superintendent's office and would like someone from that office to attend the meeting. So, my first question is, are you available after school tomorrow?

"I have an assessment meeting after school tomorrow," I replied, "but I'll reschedule it. There's nothing more important to me right now."

"I'm so sorry this is happening," she said. "I can't imagine what you're feeling. I'm not sure the Fords know what to think or who to believe...I think this is their way of looking for answers and for a direction to go."

"Thank you," I said. "But by now the word is getting out that I supposedly gave jewelry to Nora, and I'm sure there's a court of public opinion going on even as we speak."

"Don't be so sure," she said. "Everyone connected with this school knows you and your integrity; I'm sure no one is jumping to any conclusions."

"Well, I certainly hope you're right. I can't believe this has gotten to this point. I'm sort of scared here. Do you know what will happen at the meeting...the meeting with the superintendent?"

"I don't know anything yet. I'm not sure anyone does at this point. Just know that I'll support you in every way I can. I know that Nora's lying; I just wish we could figure out why."

I thanked her, and went on with my day. Nora wasn't in school that day, which made me even more nervous. This was shaping up to be quite the nightmare.

It was far from an ordinary day. It was like I was on autopilot during most of the groups I taught, and the hours went by very slowly. By lunchtime I was feeling pretty exhausted, mostly because I hadn't slept well the night before, but also because the anxiety was beginning to wear me down.

My new short-term goal was to get through the day, and to go home and take a nap. That was about as far out as I could plan at the moment, and the promise to myself of a late-afternoon nap was the only carrot I could conjure up in my foggy brain. I did eventually catch a second wind, and actually got kind of energetic with my early afternoon groups. I would make it through the rest of the day…and home to my nap.

During the fifteen-minute afternoon recess, my phone rang. It was Mrs. Skyler; she had just finished leading a reading group in Mrs. Anders' classroom, and now the kids had gone out to recess. Normally, she would return to the Resource Room at this time, to prep for our post-recess groups. Instead, she had called me to ask if I had a few minutes to come over to Mrs. Anders' classroom. I told her I did, and took a quick walk over there.

When I walked in the room, I found Mrs. Skyler standing with Mrs. Anders; they were with a girl from the classroom named Morgan.

Mrs. Skyler said, "I have something interesting to share with you, Mr. L; I think you'll like hearing this. I was gathering up my materials, getting ready to head back to the Resource Room, when I overheard Morgan say something to Mrs. Anders. Morgan, can you tell Mr. L what you said to Mrs. Anders, please."

"I told Mrs. Anders that I think someone stole something out of my desk in the last day or two. I had a pair of earrings in a little box in my desk, and they're not in there anymore. I think someone took them."

I asked her, "What do the earrings look like, Morgan?"

"They're little blue dolphins," she replied. "I was showing them to some of the girls in the classroom two days ago, and then I put them way inside my desk, to hide them. I guess I didn't hide them well enough. I meant to bring them home with me yesterday, but I forgot to."

I looked at Mrs. Skyler, who was smiling a 'happy-for-you' smile as she looked back at me. She said, "Thank you for giving up a few minutes of your recess, Morgan. We'll see what we can do about helping you find your earrings. I have a feeling we'll be able to find them … we'll let you know."

After Morgan left, Mrs. Skyler added, "And wouldn't you know it, Nora's desk is right across the aisle from Morgan's."

"I can't even begin to tell you how relieved I am," I said, "and how much I appreciate you solving this mystery. It all makes sense now. Nora had a choice between confessing that she stole the earrings, or making up a lie to say they were a gift from someone. From me. Don't I feel special that I was the person that jumped to mind? Thank you, Lisa. So much."

"I'm happy I could help solve the mystery."

I swung by the office to share the news with Mrs. Carrier, and asked her how we should proceed. She smiled, and suggested that I should be the one to call Mrs. Ford with the new revelation. I thanked her and said that it would be my pleasure to make that call. And, to tell you the truth … it was.

A MATTER OF PRINCIPAL

Travis Solera fidgeted in his seat, totally bored with today's science lesson on Copernicus and his theories.

"As if the world revolves around this guy or something," he chuckled to himself.

He drummed impatiently with his fingertips on his blank notebook page. Putting his elbow on his desk and his chin in his palm, he started doodling on the page with his pencil. He made a fat line across the bottom of the page with the side of his lead, decided it would make a great ground, then penciled in a few rocks and a tree. He drew a large bird, then had it pull a long worm up out of the ground. He added some daisy-shaped clouds and an oblong sun. He shone lines of sunshine in all directions, with a generous amount falling on the bird. As a finishing touch, he wrote 'THIS CLASS SUCKS' inside the biggest cloud, and began re-tracing the letters.

"I'll just save this to the cloud," he mused to himself as he re-traced.

The girl who sat across the aisle from him, his friend Rachel, giggled loudly when she looked over and saw what Travis had written. He gave her a quick look of disapproval, and flashed her a silent 'shush' sign. He then turned his eyes back toward the front of the room, and saw Mrs. Thomas coming down the aisle toward him.

"What's that you've got there that everyone finds so funny, Travis?" she asked.

His heart jumped, but his mind went right into damage control. He couldn't let her see what he had written.

"Gee, I'm sorry Mrs. Thomas," he said without taking his eyes from hers, while turning the notebook over on his desk. "I think…my stomach gurgled, and I guess that *was* kind of funny." Was there a chance she wouldn't ask to see the drawing?

"Let me see that drawing, please," she said, reaching her hand toward him.

"I didn't eat breakfast this morning, and sometimes that makes my stomach get all gurgley," he said, as he slowly pulled the notebook down into his lap.

"Hand me that notebook, young man."

Travis swallowed hard. He looked past her for a moment and saw the rest of the class turned around in their seats, watching silently. He looked up again at Mrs. Thomas, and was startled by the hardened expression on her face. The top of her hair shimmered in a patch of sunlight as she stood over him.

"No, I'd rather not," he said, looking her right in the eye.

There were a few gasps, and then some loud chuckles from his mates. Mrs. Thomas was taken aback for a moment, but the laughter in the room brought her right back into focus.

"Who do you think you are?" she fumed. "Give me that notebook right NOW!"

Travis didn't move... he just sat there looking up at her. Because she had taken one more step toward him, she was even more obscured by the sunlight that engulfed her head and shoulders.

"Last chance," she warned, re-extending her hand toward him.

He looked down into his lap, paused, then slowly and meticulously tore the top few pages from his notebook, folded them once and stuffed them into his pants pocket. He looked up, handed her the notebook, and gave her a bit of a smile.

He sat quietly on the bench in the main office, watching Mrs. Downing going about her work. Mr. Crenshaw would be ready to see him in just a few minutes. Despite being a special education student with autism, with supposed social skill issues, Travis had never been sent to the principal's office before. He was surprised to discover... he really liked it!

He wondered if it'd be okay to joke around with Mrs. Downing a bit, but she was busy doing paperwork, so he stayed quiet. He began replaying the classroom incident in his mind; maybe he should have torn the drawing in half... no, into little pieces...

Mr. Crenshaw was ready for him. Summoned to the foot of the throne.

"Well, Mr. Solera, this is quite a surprise. I never thought I'd see you in my office for disciplinary reasons," he said, while peering over the top of his reading glasses. "This incident report from Mrs. Thomas doesn't sound like the Travis I know."

Travis looked down at his shoes. Damn... the laces got muddy from playing soccer at recess.

"She says you weren't paying attention during her science lesson, that you made some kind of drawing, and that you wouldn't give it to her when she asked for it. Sound about right?"

"Yes sir," he said, then looked back down at his shoes and frowned.

"She also said that you were disrespectful to her in front of the whole class."

"She's lying," he said to himself. "It was *not* the whole class... Eddie Ducowitz isn't even here today."

"Yes sir," he said.

"Travis, this isn't like you. You're an excellent student, very responsible and respectful usually, so I'm going to be lenient this time. I'm not going to ask you to give us that drawing, because doodling some picture isn't why you were sent to the office. But being disrespectful to staff *is* why you were sent here, and that's never okay. I'd like to think you'll make much better choices in the future."

"Like a hundred years from now, when we all have spaceships and death-ray guns?" he joked to himself.

"Yes sir," he said. "I didn't mean to be disrespectful. I just thought the drawing was my private business and that she didn't have the right to take it. It was... the principle!"

"Yeah, it was your fault!" he chuckled to himself.

"Well, here's what we're going to do. I want you to write a letter of apology to Mrs. Thomas, right now, and then give it to her when you return to class. And, you'll be spending the 2:45 recess in detention with Mr. Lowry. So, you sit right there and write her a nice apology note... and you need to mean what you say!"

"I will, Mr. Crenshaw," he lied.

He thought for a few moments, then wrote: *Dear Mrs. Thomas -- I'm sorry you asked me to give you my notebook and I didn't think I had to. Because it was my own personal business. It will never happen again. Sinceerly, Travis Solera*

Mr. Crenshaw looked over the note, smiled then grimaced slightly, nodded his approval and sent him back to class.

When he got to his classroom, Travis walked quickly up to Mrs. Thomas near the whiteboard and handed her the note. He slapped some silent low fives as he walked to his seat at the back of the room. Mrs. Thomas said nothing, stopping her lesson just long enough to unfold the note and give it a read. It was obvious from her frown that she was not satisfied with the apology. No sir, not even close.

Returning to the lesson, she found herself shooting occasional glances back toward Travis, hoping to catch him doing something, anything, wrong. But he sat angelically with his hands folded, listening to her every word. It might have been her imagination, or perhaps it was the sunlight that was now slanting across his face, throwing shadows across his features. But she could have sworn he winked at her.

SAVING ENDANGERED STUDENTS

Barbara Parrish was in her classroom one morning, preparing her lesson plans for the day, when her phone rang.

"Good morning…"

"May I speak with Barbara Parrish, please?"

"This is Barbara. Who's calling?"

"My name is Margaret Cummings; I'm an investigator at the Pierce County Prosecuting Attorney's office. Do you have a few minutes, Mrs. Parrish?"

"Miss Parrish… and yes, I do. How can I help you?"

"May I ask, is Connor Jurgensen one of your students?"

"Yes, he's one of my special education students. I'm not his mainstream classroom teacher, but I do work with him on a pull-out basis twice a day here in my Resource Room."

"Yes, I'm aware of that. I spoke with his classroom teacher, Miss Schramm, and she steered me toward you."

"May I ask what this is about?"

"Connor has been accused of severely injuring his neighbor's cat, by shooting it with a bow and arrow. The neighbor is pressing charges. Two kids from the neighborhood saw him do it, and Connor has admitted that he did shoot the arrow. There's going to be an arraignment in juvenile court on these charges, and we're looking for some specific pieces of information from teachers and staff members at your school as we prepare for the arraignment."

"Oh my," Barbara responded. "What kind of information? How can I help?"

"Before I answer you," Margaret replied, "I want you to understand that depending on how this case unfolds, if it goes to court you might be subpoenaed to appear as an expert witness."

"Um, okay," said Barbara. "I'm not sure how I could be an expert witness, but I'll be willing to help any way I can."

"Thank you," Margaret said. "Connor's lawyer and parents are contending that, because he's a special education student, he didn't understand the seriousness of what he was doing. It's their contention that he isn't able to judge right from wrong, or to understand that animals feel pain or suffering."

"And you want my opinion as to whether that's the case?" Barbara asked.

"That's part of what I'm asking," replied Margaret. "But also, I'd like to find out if there are any parts of your curriculum where you teach things like caring about others, or caring for animals, or discerning right from wrong? I'm talking actual lessons that hopefully even have permanent product examples of his participation and understanding... such as written assignments he's produced that you might have in your possession. And yes, I'm also interested in hearing your opinion."

"Well first of all," Barbara said, "let me say that Connor's special ed eligibility designation is 'learning disabled'. You might already know, and I would imagine this would be very important for you to use in your preparation, that being learning disabled is *not* an indication of limited intelligence or poor comprehension. Not at all. I've found over the years that the concept of a student being learning disabled is very misunderstood by the general public. A learning disability simply means a student has a significant gap between where his cognitive scores tell us he should be achieving academically, and where he actually performs in academic areas. In fact, sometimes students with learning disabilities can actually have IQs well above the average range."

"That kind of information," Margaret replied, "would be one of the reasons we need your expertise. As you say, that probably is misunderstood by most people, myself included. Can you elaborate on that a little further, please?"

"Yes," Barbara continued. "Maybe the best way to elaborate is to use an example. Let's say there's a student who has an overall IQ of 110, which would be 10 points above average. Already we can see that intelligence and comprehension are not challenges for this kid. That IQ score of 110 indicates to us that he should have the cognitive ability to score at *about* that same level in all academic areas. So, a student's cognitive scores…their IQ…sets the bar for what we would expect them to be able to achieve academically. If they achieve academically well below the bar in any given subject areas, and if that gap is significant enough, then they would qualify as learning disabled in that particular subject, or subjects. So, being eligible for special ed services as learning disabled by no means indicates a low level of intelligence or an inability to understand concepts."

"Thank you for explaining that so clearly," Margaret said. "How big would the gap have to be in order to qualify as learning disabled?"

"If a student scores more than one and a half standard deviations below his or her IQ in any given academic area, he or she would qualify for special ed services as learning disabled in that specific subject. One and a half standard deviations works out to be twenty-two and a half points. So, if he or she scores twenty-three or more points lower than their overall IQ in any subject area, that gap would be considered 'significant', and they would qualify for services as learning disabled in that subject. There are other considerations that could enter into the eligibility decision, but the discrepancy between IQ and academic achievement is generally the basis for the decision."

"This is all very useful and important information, Miss Parrish," Margaret said. "Can you tell me what Connor's IQ and academic scores are?"

"Yes," Barbara replied. "I pulled out his file as we've been speaking, and I have Connor's scores right in front of me. Now, keep in mind that for the intelligence assessment, the IQ assessment, the average range is between 85 and 115, with 100 being exactly average. Every student's overall IQ is broken down into two main sub-areas: their 'Performance IQ', which assesses their ability to visualize and understand concrete information and situations; and their 'Verbal IQ', which is more their ability to work with abstract information, and to use their verbal memory to access information they've learned in the past. Connor's performance IQ is 101, and his verbal IQ is 105. The average of those two scores tells us that his overall 'Full Scale' IQ is 103. So, Connor's IQ is slightly above average.

"Now, I should tell you…when I say a learning disability is not correlated with low intelligence, there would be one exception. That would be if the student's IQ is very low in the first place. A kid with a very low IQ could then also have a significant gap between their intelligence level and their academic scores, and become eligible for special education with a learning disability. That would be the one variation where someone could perhaps argue that a learning-disabled kid has challenges with intelligence and comprehension. But as we just discussed, Connor's IQ is above average, so that exception totally doesn't apply to him. But I thought you should know about any sort of exceptions that might be brought up, and why they would not apply to Connor."

"I appreciate that very much," said Margaret. "But now I'm curious, and this is a bit of an aside; if a student's IQ is very low, wouldn't they qualify as something like mentally retarded? Pardon me if I'm using an antiquated term there."

"No, it's okay," Barbara replied. "And it's a good question. Yes, there would be a limit as to how low a kid's IQ could be for a learning disability to still apply. If his or her IQ is below 70, which is two standard deviations below average, the option of a learning disability gets taken off the table and their eligibility would become what is now referred to as an 'intellectual disability'."

"Thank you for explaining that to me," Margaret said. "And thank you for the effort to try to think of arguments that might be made with regard to special education eligibility. That's not necessary, but I do appreciate it...since I don't know much about special ed regulations."

"You're very welcome," said Barbara. "I have to say, we're touching on one of my pet peeves here...people using a special ed label to enable kids, or to hold them to a much lower standard than others. Or in this instance, representing Connor as having very low intelligence just because he's a special education student. It's especially egregious in this case, saying that this learning-disabled boy didn't comprehend what he was doing, since there *is* no correlation between his learning disability and lack of intelligence or comprehension."

"I understand how you feel, especially since you work with special needs students every day," Margaret said. "Okay, can we take a look at your experiences with Connor in your academic groups, please. What are your general impressions of him as a student? And, have there been any lessons on distinguishing right from wrong, or caring about people or animals, like I mentioned earlier?"

"Well, first here's some background context you might want to know. Connor was new to the district and to our school as of mid-October, so I've only known him for about five months now. He joined into Resource

Room groups that had already been together for a while. He did have some turbulence at first; I saw a lot of posturing from him, like he was a tough guy…you know, too cool for school. And there were some playground issues as well in his first few weeks…a few pushing and shoving incidents. But after about the first month or so, he seemed to settle in rather nicely."

"Thank you for that background information," Margaret said. "That is good to know."

"As for his groups here in the Resource Room," Barbara continued, "he's served in special education only in math and written language. In terms of math, he only qualifies in the specific area of math computation, where his academic achievement score is 80. That means his skills in adding, subtracting, multiplying and dividing are significantly low. And they are…he still uses many primary-level strategies to solve those types of problems, and that impacts his computation skills. We've been working on learning more grade-appropriate strategies since he arrived, but he still has a lot of catching up to do. His math reasoning skills, on the other hand, are solid. He scored 96 in math reasoning. This indicates that his math problem-solving skills are pretty close to average. Now, as for lessons in math that might have touched on things like caring for people or animals, or for distinguishing right from wrong in the world…we don't really go there in math lessons. Math is more about concrete, left-brain stuff."

"That makes sense," said Margaret.

"Okay, he doesn't qualify for services in reading, but I have those numbers right in front of me, so I might as well share them with you. His reading fluency is right about at his grade-level benchmark; he read 140 words correctly per minute in his spring screening, and the benchmark for 5th graders in the spring is 143 words per minute. And his reading comprehension score was 104, which is solidly in the average range. So, reading, and understanding what he reads, are also relative strengths for him.

"As for writing…when he first arrived at our school, Connor was reluctant to put forth the effort to write, and apparently he'd been reluctant for some time. This is a fairly common thing with some intermediate-aged kids…especially boys. As written assignments get longer, in grades 4 and beyond, willingness to do all that work starts to fade with some kids. Part of the job of any teacher, perhaps especially special education teachers, is to motivate and inspire kids to always give you their best efforts. Connor works hard for me, and I've seen skills well above what his scores on the assessment show us. He's actually capable of doing close to grade-level written work, when he's inspired to do so.

"He and I have forged a nice bond…he knows that I care about him, and maybe more-importantly, that I have high expectations for him. And because I expect a lot from him, and because I believe in him, he works hard for me as a result. He wants me to be proud of him.

"And actually," Barbara said, looking up at the clock, "I'm sorry, but I need to go. It's almost time for opening bell and I have some more prep work to do. But I do have time after school today… I'd be happy to talk more then, if that works for you?"

"That would be great," Margaret replied. "What time should I call?"

"I'll be free by 4:15," said Barbara. "Does that work for you?

"Yes, it does.

"Great. In the meantime, I'll look through Connor's work folder to try to find examples of what you're asking for. I have one assignment in mind already that might be very useful to you."

"That's terrific," Margaret said. "I'll call you at 4:15 then. Thank you so much for being so helpful already. Have a nice day."

"You too, Mrs. Cummings."

Holy Moly. The allegations surprised Barbara quite a bit. She thought back to October, to Connor's first few weeks at the school. As a new kid at the school, he did get into a few squabbles and shoving matches with other boys. Barbara had been involved in two such instances, where she had been called upon to de-escalate Connor's anger. But she also recalled that she had been very impressed by how receptive he was to working with her to calm down, and to turn his day around in a positive fashion. She really thought that Connor was a good kid...a good person. She wanted to think that when he injured that cat, he'd made an impulsive, terrible decision... maybe not thinking the arrow would actually hit the cat. That, she could envision. Him making that choice if it involved pre-meditation and bad intent was hard for her to even imagine.

She also thought back to the afternoon when she had met his parents. At that time, Connor had been at the school for a couple of weeks, and Barbara had thought it would be a good idea to invite both parents in, to introduce herself, and to talk about the plan going forward. Connor was still in the midst of having some conflicts with peers, and Barbara wanted to speak with them about developing a unified plan to help him become less angry and aggressive.

She closed her eyes, and sadly shook her head as she recalled the meeting. She remembered that his parents had spent almost the entire twenty-or-so minutes talking about how disappointed they were with Connor...how he was nothing but a stupid, lazy loser who would never amount to anything. They had actually said those things...thank goodness Connor hadn't been there! She could only begin to imagine how they talked to him and treated him at home. They also had said that for him, going to school was a complete waste of time, but that it at least got him out of their house for most of the day. They were, she remembered thinking, perhaps the most insensitive, self-centered and uncaring people she had ever met. She also recalled thinking, 'Gosh, now that I've met you and see who Connor has for role-models at home, he's actually remarkably well-adjusted'.

After her conversation with Mrs. Cummings, the day went by uneventfully. Connor wasn't at school, which didn't surprise her. She knew, and abided by, the knowledge that she couldn't discuss this issue with others. At 4:10, she shut her classroom door. By 4:16, the discussion had started back up.

"As for academic lessons we've done teaching right from wrong, or regarding caring about animals," Barbara said, "like I'd said this morning, math doesn't lend itself very well to that. But work we've done in our *writing* group recently might be more what you're looking for. We completed a lengthy writing project last month about saving endangered species. We spent a lot of time researching and writing about what we humans can do to help save endangered animals. I have his written work in front of me here…the organizational brainstorm pages, the rough drafts, the revisions, and the final draft that he typed and printed out. I think this entire written assignment might be helpful to you."

"That sounds very interesting," said Margaret. "Tell me more about the project, please."

"We worked on the project for about three weeks. First, the students all went online, and found an endangered animal they wanted to write about…Connor chose the black rhinoceros. After everyone made their choices, the group discussed what it means to be 'endangered', and what could cause animals to become endangered. Then they all made a list of causes, ones they'd want to use in their report. Connor's list has: diseases, pollution, de-forestation, being hunted by humans, and being hunted and eaten by other animals.

"Next, we brainstormed some ways humans could help animals overcome each of the causes on that first list. Connor's list was: diseases: give them medicine, pollution: stop polluting our rivers and air, de-foresta-tion: make it illegal to cut down trees to build buildings where the forest used to be, hunted by humans: make it illegal to hunt animals on the endangered species list. He couldn't think of a way to keep other animals from eating endangered animals.

"The next part of the assignment was to make a list of all the reasons it would be important for humans to help endangered species. Connor's list was: so they don't disappear from the face of the earth, because if they die their babies won't have parents to take care of them, and because if they're cool animals to look at, we wouldn't be able to look at them anymore.

"Then, after generating lists for those three main ideas, each student wrote a rough draft of their report, using a writing template they've learned this year. When they finished their rough draft, they did some editing for grammar and spelling, and some revising. Then they got to type up and print out their final draft. Want me to read you Connor's paper, his final draft? It's just a page and a half long."

"Yes, please, if you don't mind."

"I don't mind at all. Actually, I'd like you to hear this.

"Saving Endangered Species, by Connor Jurgensen. 'Do you know why animals become endangered? First, their habitats are being destroyed because humans cut down forests to build shopping malls. We also build houses for people to live in, and then animals don't have a habitat to live in. Next, people hunt animals, and so endangered animals get wiped out. Other animals hunt endangered animals too, but they have to because they have to eat to survive. Finally, the rivers and lakes of the world are getting very polluted, and endangered animals drink that water and get sick and die. The air is polluted too, and all animals have to breathe, so that makes them real sick, too. As you can see, there are a lot of reasons animals become endangered.

'There are many reasons we should try to save endangered animals. First, if animals die, their babies wouldn't have parents. Without parents, they would die too and make things even worse. Next, many animals are cool to look at, because they are colorful or big. If they all die, we wouldn't be able to look at them anymore, and that would be too bad. Finally, how would you like it if you were endangered? Wouldn't you want someone to try to save you? I would. Clearly, there are many reasons to try to save endangered animals.

'There are lots of ways we can save endangered animals. First, we can make it illegal to cut down forests and jungles to put up houses and shopping malls. We should put up houses and shopping malls some-where else. Second, we can make it illegal to hunt animals that are en-dangered. In places where it's already illegal, we should put more police so they can arrest people who break the law. Third, we should all stop polluting the rivers, lakes, and the air. We can do that by recycling and carpooling, and by getting rid of smokestacks. As you can see, there are many things we can do to try to save endangered animals.

'I'd like to tell you about one cool endangered animal, the black rhi-noceros. First, black rhinos live in eastern and southern Africa. Their habitats are open plains, dry forests, and savannas, which are grasslands. Next, they are herbivores, which means they eat plants. That means they don't kill other animals, so they are peaceful animals. They eat leaves, bushes, and fruit. Finally, there are only about 2,500 black rhinos left in the world. Their lifespan is 40 to 50 years, if they don't get killed by humans, pollution, or disease. Clearly, black rhinos need our help to survive.'

"So, there you have it … that's his report. It sure seems to me that he understands that animals have feelings, and that they need to be treated kindly."

"I agree," said Margaret. "Frankly, that's exactly what I was looking for. Would I be able to get that report from you, please? I would need the original, since it's going to be used as evidence. I could get it back to you when this whole process is over with."

"Absolutely," replied Barbara. "I'll make a copy to put in his writing file, so there'll be no hurry to get the original report back to me."

"Thank you," said Margaret. "I have to ask … are those Connor's own thoughts, or did you help him come up with those?"

"Those are his thoughts. There were many thoughts shared out loud during our brainstorming sessions, but students all decided on their own what they wanted to say, and totally wrote the reports on their own. I only gave input about editing, punctuation, and grammar."

"Are there any other examples of his understanding of right versus wrong, or of why cruelty to animals is wrong?"

"No, not anything I see in our written assignments. But I hope the work we did on endangered species was, or will be, helpful. I think it's safe to say that Connor showed he has a deep appreciation of animals, and concern for them if they're suffering. Oh, speaking of which, may I ask…how's the cat doing?"

"The cat's doing fine," said Margaret, "but it'll take some time before it fully recovers."

"Thank goodness it's going to be okay," said Barbara. "That's great for everyone involved, including Connor."

"I agree," Margaret replied. "So, would it be okay for me to send a courier over tomorrow morning to pick up the report?"

"Absolutely. I'll leave the original draft up in the main office with the receptionist. I'll put it in a manilla envelope. Should I put your name on the envelope?"

"Yes, please put 'to be delivered to Margaret Cummings'. That's all you need to write on the envelope, the courier will get it to me. Oh, and may I also get a copy of the results of his IQ assessment and his academic scores? I don't need the original of those…a copy will do."

"I'll be happy to do that," Barbara said. "His IQ data and his academic scores are all in his Special Education Evaluation document. I'll put a copy in the envelope with his writing project."

"Thank you," said Margaret. "I'll contact you if it turns out that we'll need to subpoena you, or if I need to discuss this further with you. Thank you again, you've been a very big help. Take care."

"You too, Mrs. Cummings. Goodbye."

The following week, Barbara received a call from Mrs. Cummings to let her know that Connor's lawyer and parents were no longer going to pursue the 'he isn't intelligent enough to know right from wrong', and the 'he didn't know animals have feelings' defense. Her involvement was over. Connor pleaded guilty and was put on probation. He had to attend weekly counselling sessions, but he could still attend school, so that was very good. He was also put under close parental supervision at home for the times of day he wasn't at school.

Barbara knew the 'close parental supervision' part wasn't such a great outcome for him, knowing what she knew about his home life. She also knew he would need help recovering from the terrible decision he'd made. In his black rhino report, he had written, 'If you were endangered, wouldn't you want someone to help you? I would'. Barbara was intent on being that someone; and doing whatever it took to help Connor get through this dark time in his life. The best thing she could do for him was to be a positive, encouraging, and supportive role model every day. He sure needed one.

THE JOURNEY FROM
INSTITUTION TO
CLASSROOM

The other night, one of my friends and I were at a tavern having a few microbrews. He knew I was originally an east coast guy with an undergrad degree in marketing, and asked me how the heck I ended up becoming an elementary school special ed teacher in Tacoma, Washington. I told him it was kind of a long story. But he was curious, so we ordered up another round and I told him about the long, strange journey.

It started at the University of Connecticut, where I was getting my Bachelor's Degree in Business Administration. I was in my junior year, working hard at my studies of course, but also working two or three jobs to make ends meet. I worked at a dorm called Keller House as a pot washer; the job didn't pay money, but it gave me three meals a day, and a place on campus to sort of *belong* to. Some of my best friends in the world today were fellow kitchen workers and wait staff there, so that job was totally worth working at.

I also worked at a local pub as a bartender, being lucky enough to be there one night when the owner and the bartender got into a yelling match, with the bartender getting fired. The guy had been stealing from the cash register, apparently. The owner walked over to our table, which was close to the bar, to vent a bit about how hard it was to find good help. I asked if he might be looking to hire a new barkeep. He asked me if I knew how to tend bar, and I lied to him and said yes. It was a shot and beer joint anyway, and I knew how to pour glasses of beer and fill shot glasses. That job was very worthwhile, too...good tips and lots of good memories. It just goes to show you, and we'll be seeing this again in my journey, that sometimes being in the right place at the right moment in time can make a big difference. Serendipity. Sometimes the benefit is a short-term nicety, like a few years of tending bar. But sometimes a chance occurrence can plant a seed that grows fruit for a lifetime.

One morning I was having breakfast at Keller House. One of the guys at the table, named Chris, was talking about his job, where he was about to give his two-week notice. He said he'd had enough, that the work was just not for him. One of us at the table asked him what kind of job it was...we were all probably in that 'always looking for an extra side job' mode...and he filled us in. The job was working as a tutor at a place called Mansfield Training School. It was an institution, the kind you'd see in movies like *One Flew Over the Coocoo's Nest* or *The Dream Team*. This was back in 1978, before they had started closing institutions.

Actually, deinstitutionalization was already happening at that time, but institutions were not really being closed down yet. There wasn't a plan B that was readily available, so closing such places was not yet in the cards. Our country was just not ready for that to happen.

Anyway, Chris said he worked in one particular cottage (which sounded kind of quaint, but wasn't...it turned out to be one of many little concrete buildings at Mansfield), and that his job was working with one specific twenty-two-year-old resident named Stevie. Chris wasn't an employee of the institution...he worked directly for Stevie's parents. They lived in New York City, and had placed Stevie at Mansfield when he was a youngster. Schools didn't have the resources or expertise in those days to work successfully with kids like Stevie, so he was sent off to live at Mansfield ... for the rest of his life.

Now in those days, some people even placed their children with Down's Syndrome in places like that, or kids with other such benign conditions. Apparently, society didn't know any better at the time ... shame on society. But this young man, Stevie, was an extremely impacted individual. It was understandable, in those days, why he needed to be in an institution, especially since schools were not yet ready to effectively help him.

Anyway, so Chris started telling us about the job. He'd been hired to go to the training school three days a week for two hours a day to work with Stevie. Chris got to choose between a number of activities: they could play a game together, like bounce a ball or shoot hoops, or take a walk around the institution's grounds together. Or he could take Stevie off the grounds to walk around our nearby U-Conn campus. The parents were wealthy, and gave him a nice little hourly wage, and paid for all food and beverages... he just needed to get receipts.

I became instantly intrigued. I asked Chris if he'd be willing to pass along my name and phone number to the parents when he put in his notice. Chris said he would do that, and that offering them a potential replacement would help him feel a little better about giving his notice. No one else at the table was interested, so I thought I really might have a chance of getting the job. A few days later, I received a call from Stevie's father, and after a long conversation, he offered me the job.

Now keep in mind (serendipity) that if I wasn't at that exact table for breakfast at the right time that morning, I wouldn't have ended up working at that institution, and I probably wouldn't have ended up becoming a special education teacher, which turned into a more than 25-year career for me.

The following week, I had to go over to Mansfield to fill out 'guest employee' paperwork, or whatever it was called. I had also made arrangements to visit Stevie's cottage...to meet him and his fellow residents. I was told that I would be given an orientation training by one of the supervisors at the cottage. It was not the kind of place, apparently, you could just walk in off the street and work at. There were many rules, procedures, and frankly, dangers to learn about. Stevie's parents were nice enough to even pay me for my time to attend the training; they knew better than I did what I was about to get myself into.

I arrived at the cottage one afternoon for my orientation training. When I got out of my car in the parking lot, I was greeted by an oppressive, pungent smell that reminded me of maybe a mixture of gasoline and disinfectant. It was nasty, and it of course got nastier as I approached the cottage.

When I went inside, the first person I came to was a resident...a young man with a football helmet on. A New York Giants helmet. I said hello, and he said nothing. So, I moved farther into the large room, where there were several adult men sitting around or walking about. I noted that some of the men were very verbal, some of them talking to no one in particular, and others weren't doing much talking or socializing. I knew I had to find the supervisor, or at least an employee who was working that day. But the room was full of men between the ages of twenty and sixty, some obviously residents, but many pretty ordinary-looking guys at first glance. So, scanning the room, it was hard for me to tell staff from resident. It took a minute, since I also blended in with the background, but one staff member noticed me. It was the supervisor who was going to give me my orientation training. When he saw me, he quickly walked over and introduced himself. Robert was a very nice man, and quickly put me at ease... as much as possible, anyway.

Robert suggested we start by taking a walking tour of the cottage, so he could introduce me to the two other staff members, and to the residents. But first, he introduced me to Stevie. Before that day, I had never met anyone with any sort of mental disability that I knew of; no one with Down's Syndrome, autism, or any type of (what at that time was called) mental retardation. So, meeting Stevie was quite alarming. Here was this young man with profound autism and severe mental retardation, flapping his arms wildly while pacing back and forth in front of me as we were introduced. When I said hello, and that it was nice to meet him, he jabbered phrases like 'Stevie good', 'Stevie want food', and alarmingly, 'Stevie bad, tie me up'. I didn't know what the hell else to say at that moment. After several uncomfortable moments of silence, Robert suggested that we continue on with our tour. As Stevie and I parted ways, I told him I was looking forward to seeing him the following week; Stevie said nothing and wandered off.

Robert and I moved on. He introduced me to some other residents, and pointed out some others that weren't capable of being introduced. There were three residents I still vividly recall from this part of the tour. One of the young men I was introduced to had closely-cropped black hair, with an unusual oval-shaped bald track around the top of his head. It looked as if he was wearing a bald headband...or like a halo had dropped onto his head and snuffed out the hair it touched. I remarked to myself that the guy sure had an unusual balding pattern. The mystery was solved a few minutes later, when I watched as he put his forehead against a wall, spun his body around and turned his head full-circle against the wall, over and over. Apparently, I thought to myself, he'd been doing that for a *very* long time. Along similar lines, I noticed the Giants fan banging his helmeted head against the concrete wall. That was one well-placed helmet. But my introduction to Randy was the most memorable of all. The other residents...I wouldn't end up remembering their names, other than Stevie's. But I'll always remember Randy's.

Robert walked me over to within a few feet of him, and told me to watch out, because Randy *bites*. I told him I understood. Robert told me I probably didn't fully understand; he meant that Randy bites. He called one of the nearby residents over and asked him to show us where Randy had bitten him. This guy had a huge chunk missing out of the back of his freshly-healed bicep. Yikes. I wrote down 'Randy bites…don't point finger at Randy, or get too close to him', or something like that. And I underlined those notes several times. Randy.

Robert then introduced me to the two guys that were working that day, but let me know that the staff rotated a lot, so there'd be many others to meet. He showed me where various supplies were stored, things like games and sports equipment, paper towels, a mop and bucket, a first aid kit, a fire extinguisher, and the like. He also showed me where to get a 'visitor' badge, and told me I would need to always wear one when I was in the cottage or on the grounds with Stevie.

I also learned how and where to sign Stevie out if we left the cottage…and how to indicate if we were going to leave the institution's grounds. I asked Robert if they needed any more information if I was going to take him off the grounds. He told me that as long as I logged him out on their chart, I could take him anywhere I wanted. I don't think they were concerned I might decide to keep him, or kidnap him or anything.

I showed up for my first day of work the following week, and signed Stevie out of the cottage. I wanted to take a short walk around the grounds with him so we could talk…so I could get to know him, and he could get to know me. I definitely wanted to find out how much communication could happen between the two of us, and if he would consistently be able and willing to follow my directions. At the top of my list was to discover if he would stay with me as we went on a walk, or if he'd wander off when we went places together. I certainly wanted to find this out while we were on the secure campus of Mansfield's grounds. My biggest initial fear was eventually taking him off the institution's grounds, and then losing him. That would not be good.

Over the course of my first several days working with Stevie, I learned that I could totally trust him to stay with me when we went for walks together. I considered these to be 'test' days, and was pleased to find out that he was not a runner or a wanderer. In fact, he became almost imprinted on me…he pretty much walked right at my side wherever we went. I even drove him in my car to a few different locations on the Mansfield grounds, so we could practice getting out of the car, going for a walk, and then getting back in the car. There was never a problem that would indicate that I would ever be in danger of losing him.

These 'tests', of course, were trial runs to simulate us leaving Mansfield and going elsewhere, and going elsewhere was my preference for our activities together. Stevie's father indicated that it was his wife's and his preference as well. They wanted Stevie to get as much exposure to 'real life' activities as possible. I never met this man, I only ever talked with him on the phone. And I only once or twice ever talked with his wife. But I could tell that they were very nice people, and that they were wracked with guilt about having put their son in an institution for his entire life. It was my intention to help in my small way, and give them the peace of mind of knowing that Stevie was in good hands.

We started to develop a repertoire of things to do while staying on Mansfield's grounds. We always took at least a short walk, to get Stevie (and myself?) out of that stinky cottage. I came up with a few activities I thought might be beneficial, such as bouncing a rubber kickball back and forth to each other, counting as we made each catch. Stevie could count to about 12, though some days he couldn't get anywhere near that high. We also often sat out on the grassy lawn behind the cottage, and I would read to him using children's picture books. I thought this might fill in some gaps from missed experiences in his life, and I was surprised to find that Stevie loved being read to. Other residents from his cottage would usually join us on the back lawn, and they all seemed to love it too. It became one of our normal activities for part of each day's agenda, if the weather was nice. We weren't able to do that reading circle thing if we were stuck inside due to rain; there was too much activity and talking going on inside the cottage.

I would send a weekly 'report' to his parents through the mail, with a brief description of each day's activities, as well as my number of hours worked, receipts, etc. His father called me one weekend, and was very emotional about my idea to read to Stevie. He and his wife loved that I was doing that…he said it made their hearts happy, and that they very much appreciated the job I was doing. That made me even more determined to give Stevie the best, most beneficial experiences I could think of.

It also planted a major seed in my mind. I remember wishing that Stevie had been much younger, so that the activities I was doing with him could have had a greater impact on his knowledge and development. I couldn't help but think…wouldn't it have been great if Stevie could have received meaningful instruction and experiences as a young boy, when his clay was still wet? Maybe he could have been saved from having to live his whole life in this dismal, unstimulating place. And, the same thought must surely apply to the hundreds of residents at Mansfield, and the tens of thousands across the country that had to spend their lives in institutions. I was new to this line of thinking, but I conjured up lofty disdain for the entire system that was in place.

I got myself a card at the local public library, and often stopped in to check out children's books. I unintentionally began to accumulate a lot of experience and information about children's literature. And I found myself wanting to find out more and more about special education services in Connecticut. I had a good friend who was a special education major at U-Conn, and borrowed some of her introductory textbooks about working with students with autism and mental retardation. My business courses that semester allowed me one outside-of-business elective class, so I took an introductory class in special education. The more I read and studied, the more I became convinced that people like Stevie should be given a chance to learn and grow in the real world, not stashed away in the barren world of some institution. I didn't realize it at the time, but more and more seeds were starting to take root in my mind.

Then came a significant day in my job with Stevie, in more ways than one as it turned out. I finally felt comfortable enough to take him off the Mansfield grounds for the first time, for a 'field trip' to the U-Conn campus. My plan that day was simple: make a quick stop on campus to buy us each an ice cream cone, then eat the cones while sitting next to Mirror Lake, then go right back to Mansfield. It sounded like a good plan at the time.

There was a particular dairy bar in the School of Agriculture portion of campus that was famous for serving up delicious ice cream. We went inside the red barn-shaped building, and then stood in line together, waiting our turn to order our cones. As we stood in line, I was very watchful of our surroundings. This was Stevie's first time out in public with me, and I wanted to see how he would do in the new environment around some strangers, and how they would do with him.

It was, of course, readily evident to even casual observers that Stevie was 'different'. His arms were almost always flailing and flapping, and he pretty regularly mumbled out loud to himself in 'Stevie' language. I wanted to make sure he and the folks in the dairy bar were all feeling comfortable with one another. I was happy to find that everyone seemed fine and relaxed.

The time waiting in line was uneventful, which was great. When we got to the counter, I ordered our cones. I turned away from Stevie for a few moments to address the cashier and pay; it was then that I heard several voices all at once express various cries of dismay. Stevie had decided he needed to pee, so he unzipped and did so, right there at the front of the line.

Yikes. I was of course very shocked, and immediately apologetic to everyone in the room. I offered to clean up the pee if they would give me some paper towels or a mop and bucket. The wonderful folks working there said not to worry, that they would get it cleaned up. They asked the entire line to re-cue over at a different cash register, so everyone could avoid the puddle. Everybody knew there had been no intentional wrong-doing, so they just sort of took it in stride and lined up at the second cash register. I was, apparently, the only one in the room who was negatively affected. Our cones had already been made, and I had already paid, so the people behind the counter said to not worry…to go have a great afternoon and enjoy our cones. I thanked them, probably way too many times, and we left…me feeling mortified, and Stevie looking forward to eating his ice cream cone.

I learned an important lesson that day. I remember wishing that the pee-at-will incident had happened sometime previously, at Mansfield, so I could have been ready for the possibility when we went out in public. But then I realized…whenever we were at Stevie's cottage, when he needed to pee or poop, he would simply get up from our activity and walk directly into the bathroom area in the cottage and relieve himself. He had no such option at the dairy bar. So, my bad. I was just glad he hadn't needed to poop at the front of the line that day.

I came up with an idea…and made a new rule. In his daily life at the cottage, when Stevie needed to use the bathroom, I wanted him to always give me, or any staff member, a verbal cue before he headed to the bathroom. I decided that he should say just one word…'bathroom'; it was a word he could easily remember and enunciate. Pretty much all his life, whenever Stevie needed to relieve himself, he just got up and walked into the bathroom and did so. It occurred to me that if we could get him to verbalize his need to go, before he left for the bathroom, he might eventually learn to pre-emptively warn us of his need to go. That way, when he was somewhere where a toilet was not readily available, such a warning might allow us to get him to a bathroom in time.

I knew this was a lofty goal, and might take a long time to develop.

But we had time, and Stevie had nothing but time. First, we had to get him to understand what it was we wanted him to do. That, by itself, would be tricky. Then, we needed to help him get in the habit of remembering to say 'bathroom' whenever he started heading for the bathroom. Another tricky proposition…inserting a step for him to take where there had never been a step before…in his entire life.

I developed a reward system to help him remember. When he remembered to say 'bathroom' before he walked to the bathroom, he would immediately get a few M&Ms. He could even say it while he was walking toward the bathroom, as long as he said it. When he forgot to do so, we would remind him, and show him the candy he could have had if he had remembered. Stevie eventually totally understood the new system, and did occasionally remember to announce his imminent peeing and/or pooping.

But to tell you the truth, it didn't work out very well at all. In order to have actually been useful and effective, Stevie would have eventually needed to learn to give us at least a one-minute prior-to-peeing heads-up, which would have actually been the only useful benefit to this training, giving us time enough to whisk him quickly to a toilet. But it was just too much to ask of someone who had spent his entire life just walking into the bathroom without saying anything to do his business. Again, I wished I could have done this kind of training with him starting back when he was a young boy…I was sure this idea could have been successful if done when he was young. That would have been very beneficial in his life, especially as we tried to give him 'real-life' experiences outside of the institution. But now, he was too settled into his life routines to effectively learn new skills and habits.

So, the new plan became…whenever Stevie and I had plans to leave the Mansfield grounds, I would make sure he always took a bathroom break before we left his cottage, whether he felt he needed to or not. That was the best new plan I could think of.

I worked with Stevie for a little more than a year. There were some other off-institution-grounds incidents, like him accidentally knocking over a big, stacked display of boxes of chocolate Easter bunnies in a grocery store due to his arm-flailing, then stomping many of them flat trying to get out of the rubble. And one time he spilled a big plastic cup of water on my roommate's turntable in our apartment, right onto an album that was playing. And there were a few more public peeing incidents, but they occurred in parking lots or in grassy areas around the U-Conn campus…so they weren't so bad. And of course, it was always interesting to be in a public place and have him blurt out 'Stevie bad, tie me up'. He used to say that a real lot. That always brought many looks of disapproval from people within earshot.

But for each 'incident', there were dozens of positive, 'real-life' experiences for Stevie. There were even some memorably heartwarming, and sometimes even humorous, events. One that jumps to mind was a time he and I were sitting by the lake. Stevie spotted a large, white goose standing near the edge of the water, maybe forty feet from us. He got a big smile on his face, stood up, looked at me and let out some loud, joyful giggles. He then decided to run over to the goose to, I don't know, maybe pet him or something? So, there he was, running full speed toward the goose, flapping his arms and blurting loud cries of excitement. The goose suddenly became understandably alarmed, but it didn't run or fly away. No, it extended its neck up straight and tall, and started running right at Stevie as he approached, honking loudly and flapping its wings. It was like a loud, spontaneous, flapping game of chicken. It was Stevie's turn to be alarmed…he slammed on his brakes and tumbled down onto the grass trying to change direction and scramble away. The goose won that encounter by a mile.

I had grown very fond of Stevie, and I really felt he had grown fond of me as well. We became regular visitors to the campus, reading near the lake, feeding the ducks (from a distance), or strolling around eating ice cream or popcorn. I have to say…I thoroughly enjoyed our time together.

But when I entered my senior year, my course load became much more intense, and I had to quit my job working with Stevie so I could focus on my studies. I visited him at the cottage a few times, and each time I read him one of his favorite books and took a short walk with him. But eventually, the visits stopped. His parents found another student at U-Conn to take my place, and I knew Stevie was once again in good hands. I stayed in touch with his parents for a few years...Christmas cards mostly, but we eventually stopped communicating. I used to think of Stevie often, but even that faded away with time. But the experience of my time with him has resonated in my life until this day.

After graduating, I worked in the business world for a little over nine years. During that time, the sprouting seeds in my mind were becoming increasingly large blossoms, pushing aside my business goals and replacing them with visions of working with the Stevies of the world. I enrolled in a Special Education certification program at a local college, and over the last seven years of my business career I went to school nights to get my teaching degree. Eventually, the time arrived to do my student teaching, so I kicked open a new door and said goodbye to my business life.

My first student teaching gig was in a quaint little town in the Resource Room of a quaint little elementary school. That was a lovely experience, and I learned a lot from my pleasant, supportive supervising teacher. Looking back now, thank goodness I had that tranquil, beneficial placement for my first student teaching experience.

Because my second placement was in inner-city Hartford, in a self-contained classroom for students with significant behavior problems. Students from various schools in that portion of the district who were too problematic or violent to be in regular classrooms were instead bussed to this school and placed in this self-contained classroom. This was my new placement for the next fourteen weeks. Yikes. To make matters even more challenging, the teacher of this classroom, my new supervising teacher (I'll call her Kate), was someone who hated teaching and hated kids even more, especially badly-behaved kids. And if that wasn't bad enough, her nastiness was exacerbated by a contentious divorce I was told she had just been through. I felt bad for her...she was entrenched in a perfect storm of things she hated. But I felt worse for myself, knowing I was going to be immersed in the troubled waters of her storm for the next fourteen weeks.

As I got to know her a little better during that first week, the forecast got even worse. I learned that, on top of everything else, Kate was also a very unskilled teacher. And she turned out to be even meaner than I had first thought. During one of my first days there, I heard her tell one of the third-grade boys to 'drop dead' after he'd said something disrespectful to her. Yikes times a million, who would say that to a nine-year old? Kate would, apparently.

The experience over those first days made me feel like I'd been cast into a 'new-teacher' episode of the TV show Naked and Afraid. Dropped into an uninviting, uninhabitable and inhospitable location, with no resources and no one to turn to for help. But there was no way I was going to tap-out.

The eventual saving grace for me was that after the first week or so, Kate was hardly ever in the classroom anymore. She spent her days in the teachers' lounge or somewhere...she could have been out shopping or at home for all I knew. That was totally okay with me, since I didn't have to deal with her negativity any more. And, the kids loved me...I was saving them from having the wicked witch of the east as their teacher. And they could see that I actually cared about them and liked them. Kids know when someone cares about them for real. There certainly were behavior challenges, like every day, but nothing I couldn't handle.

As I got to know those students, I was appalled by their back-stories. Some lived in cars, some had a parent or two in jail, a few were victims of sexual abuse, and many came from homes that were drug-filled and dangerous. It occurred to me that for most of these kids, their time in the classroom with me was the most positive and nurturing part of their little lives. That realization made me even more angry that Kate was not supplying them with any sort of respite from their turbulent lives. After a few weeks, I started to love working with them. They had all been dealt very bad hands, and I was determined to use the remaining weeks of my placement there to help them learn that school, and life, can be full of positive experiences.

During the spring break of that Hartford placement, I flew out to Washington state to attend a career fair in Spokane. My goal for the week was simple and focused: get a teaching job somewhere near Seattle, check out the city I got hired to work in, and then fly home. During my first morning at the fair, I quickly discovered that being a male special ed teacher candidate, with solid grades and references, made me quite appealing. In those days, there apparently weren't many guys who wanted to be special ed teachers. I was actually offered two jobs there at the fair, both in the Puget Sound region of western Washington. I wanted to live in the Seattle area, so those were very appealing offers. In both cases, I would need to sit through a formal interview process later that week, but I was assured by both districts' representatives at the career fair that I would be offered the job.

I tell you that information to tell you this … when I sat down with my preferred district for the formal interview, they told me they had called all my references, but were only able to reach one of them (probably because it was spring break, and I'd mostly supplied phone numbers at schools). When I heard that, I thought to myself 'oh *please* don't let that one person be Kate'. About two seconds later, they said it was Kate they had reached, and that she had given me an excellent, glowing reference.

What? Kate had said nice things about me? I didn't for the life of me know how she could have even offered up an opinion about my teaching skills … she had almost never been in the room to see me teach. Anyway,

I did end up accepting an offer from that district. I got my first job in my new career, and I was very happy and proud of myself. I had more of my student teaching to complete, but with a job in my pocket, the pressure was off and I could simply enjoy my last few weeks.

Kate actually gave me a gift on my last day in Hartford. It was the Dr. Seuss book *Oh, the Places You'll Go!*. She wrote me a nice little note of congratulations inside the front cover, and also had all of the students sign the page as well. I have no idea when she had the opportunity to get those signatures, but she went out of her way to do so. I was very appreciative of her gift and her efforts, and I still have that book to this day. She showed caring and thoughtfulness that I'm sure she had a big supply of in her earlier teaching days…I was glad I got to see at least a little glimpse of it during my time there. It's funny how she turned out to be a significant help to me in landing my first job in my new teaching career. It just goes to show you, you can't judge a book by the outside of its cover.

I was very relieved when the fourteen weeks were over…I hadn't tapped out, and I had helped, albeit briefly, a classroom full of kids who desperately needed a teacher who cared about them and wanted them to have positive, productive lives.

My first teaching job didn't start off as I had planned. I'd always envisioned sitting down with the teacher whose job I was assuming, to go over all the schedules, forms, procedures, curriculum materials, and information about the students on my new caseload. But I got hired to work at a brand-new school…it was still having the finishing touches put on it during our late August teacher trainings. So, there *was* no previous teacher, no one to sit with and tell me how things were done. Another yikes. But things turned out just fine. The district's Director of Special Education, Janice, and the Assistant Director, Bill, were both amazingly helpful, and also arranged for me to meet up with some veteran Resource Room teachers at other schools for some job tutoring. And luckily, the paraprofessional team I was fortunate enough to work with were wonderful at what they did, as well as being wonderful people. I was lucky in every regard. Thank you, Kate.

There was some serendipity that we skipped over a few minutes ago. During my spring break trip to Spokane to attend the career fair, one of those 'right place at the right time' moments occurred inside the convention center. I had visited several district's booths, and left resumes with quite a few of them. Several were interested in me (again, that male special ed thing), but they all said that they couldn't do interviews at the career fair…they would need to get in touch with me in the next day or so to arrange an interview. But one district was interested enough to interview me on the spot. They had most of the right personnel there to do so. So, we sat inside their booth and they informally interviewed me. And they offered me a job as a resource room teacher in an elementary school. They didn't know which school it would be, but they could offer me a job in their district somewhere.

There's this 'musical chairs' thing that happens in districts toward the end of school years. When there's a job opening at a school, the district opens up the position to 'in-district' applicants first. A teacher might see the new job opportunity as better than his or her current position, so they leave their school to take that new position. Then *their* position is suddenly open, and available to in-district applicants. And so on. When the music finally stops, the school that no longer has a teacher gets the new hire. That's why they couldn't tell me which school I would work at. But that was totally okay with me; I didn't know one school from another in that district anyway. I was just happy to get a job offer.

So, I left their booth knowing I had landed a job, somewhere out near Seattle. I had never been to western Washington, except one day changing planes at Sea-Tac Airport on a trip home from Anchorage the previous summer. I had made a 'scouting' trip up to Anchorage to see if that might be a city I'd be interested in moving to (I'd planned to re-locate to somewhere geographically appealing to begin my new teaching career). I had made a short list of cities to check out…my biggest requirement was that it had to be near magnificent mountains. I had briefly considered Seattle, but it didn't make my short list because in my mind it rained too much in the Pacific Northwest.

As it turned out that day, on the way back to Connecticut from Anchorage, I had a more-than-three-hour layover at Sea-Tac, so I opted to grab a taxi and do a quick tour around the area. I figured I had time to at least check out some of the sights. As it turned out, it was a crystal clear, blue sky summer day, and Mt. Rainier was out in all its glory. It hung like a huge hologram over the beautiful countryside. I immediately rethought my short list…why was western Washington not on my list? After seeing that beautiful mountain, the Seattle area went to the very top of my list, and that's where I ended up moving to. So, if I had had a shorter layover time that afternoon, I wouldn't have left the airport. And if it hadn't been a clear day, I wouldn't have seen the mountain, and would not have even considered moving to the Pacific Northwest. So that explains the 'how did I end up in Tacoma' part of my friend's question.

Anyway, so there I was in that convention center in Spokane. I had just been offered a job across the state, near Seattle…so my goal for the week was basically accomplished. My schedule for the day had just changed on a dime. With the 'career fair' part of my mission completed, I could now leave the convention center earlier than I'd planned, go back to my hotel, check out, and make the six-hour drive across the state to go check out the city I was going to live and work in. Then all I'd need to do was go to the formal interview in a few days, sign a contract, then fly home.

It was a big convention center, so there were many routes I could have taken to get to the main exit. As it turned out, the route I chose brought me past a booth that had a huge blown-up photo of a gorgeous field of daffodils, with Mt. Rainier hologramming in the background.

I stopped for a moment to admire the beautiful photo. There was only one person inside the booth at the time, and she and I chatted a bit. She asked where I was from, and when I told her, she told me that she was from Connecticut, too. Interesting coincidence. She asked if I was looking for a job. I told her that five minutes ago I had been, but that now I was all set...I already had a job in hand. She asked what kind of job I had been seeking...

As we talked, the Director of Special Education (you met her earlier, her name is Janice) returned to the booth. We talked for a few minutes, then she asked if I had signed a contract with that other district. I told her I had not, but that the formal interview and contract-signing would happen in the next few days over in their district. She asked if I'd care to sit down and also interview with them, since they, too, had a few Resource Room positions open. I told her that I would be very willing to do that. They ended up making me the same informal offer, that I could have a job in their district, and that they could also set up a formal interview and contract-signing in the next couple of days. I told them that would be great.

So, now I apparently had a choice to make. I would be in Washington for the rest of the week, so I had time to drive over to check out both cities and get a feel for what it would be like to live and work in each. I left the convention center, checked out of the hotel and drove my rental across the state. It was a long drive, but I enjoyed checking out my new state, and I was pretty exhilarated by the events of the morning.

Man, western Washington is very different than eastern Washington. Once you cross over the pass through the Cascade Mountains, it's like entering another world, full of beautiful mountains and forests. It was obvious to me that I had made an excellent geographical choice; this was where I wanted to be.

I ended up very happily working in that second district, the Sumner School District, for several years. So, me stopping to look at the giant photo of daffodils was whatever you'd like to call it...serendipity, fortunate happenstance, good luck? But that little moment sure changed my life. As did the taxi ride. And the breakfast at Keller House. And Kate and Stevie.

As I concluded my story, I added a footnote as my friend and I finished up our beers. When I had spent that year working at Mansfield Training School, the place had always seemed archaic to me...very outdated, unstimulating, and ineffective, providing services that should have been done away with long before that time period. But looking back on it so many years later, I remind myself that it's important to look at the full scope of its existence. By the time I worked there, that institution had actually progressed in many very positive ways since its inception. When it had been founded, it had originally been called the Connecticut School for Imbeciles. Apparently, for some reason that name was too offensive to some people (go figure), so eventually it was renamed the Connecticut Training School for the Feebleminded. Good intentions, but not much better. Just considering the names that were chosen gives you major insight into how close-minded and insensitive society was during those times.

It went through more name changes over the years, eventually settling on Mansfield Training School. That name was indeed better. And the services it rendered, while bleak and unfortunate, were in fact very important and effective in supplying solutions that were otherwise not available at that time for many families, and for many men, women, boys, and girls with significant special needs.

When I worked at Mansfield, there had been close to one thousand residents, people of various ages and disabilities who were designated to live their entire lives within its walls. A decade earlier, there'd been more than 1,600 such residents, stashed away to protect society from them, or was it the other way around? But by 1991, the population was down to less than 150, and then in 1993, the institution closed its doors forever.

It took a long time, but the state eventually got it right, mostly because other, better options were finally available for everyone involved.

Anyway, my friend and I played one more game of pool, then called it a night. Tomorrow would be another day of work…teaching in an environment that was totally and wonderfully beneficial for children. The happy ending to a long, serendipity-filled journey.

THE STUDENT-
REFERRAL TEAM

"Good morning, everyone," said a smiling Principal Murdock. "We're meeting this morning to discuss Brendon Rollins from Mrs. Patterson's classroom. Mrs. Rollins, thank you for attending this Student-Referral Team meeting this morning, and Brendon thank you for coming, too!"

"We're happy to be here, Dr. Murdock," said Mrs. Rollins. "Thank you in advance for any help you can give us."

"That's what this team is all about, Natalie. We're here to help in any way we can. You know everyone here at the table, right?"

"Yes," Natalie replied, giving a smiling, quick nod to the staff members seated around the conference table, with an extra affectionate nod to Mrs. Patterson.

Dr. Murdock continued, "First of all, let me say how wonderful it is to have Brendon at our school, and your whole family in our community. I know moving to a new town and new school can be challenging at first, but I know you'll just love it here. Okay, Mrs. Patterson, please get us started. What successes and challenges have you been experiencing with Brendon?"

"Well, let me start by saying it's a pleasure having Brendon in our classroom! For the first five weeks of the school year, I didn't have any problems whatsoever with Brendon. He was doing all of his work, and doing a great job in every regard," she said, looking and smiling at Brendon. "He was participating enthusiastically in class discussions and activities, getting along great with his classmates, and being very respectful to me."

"But that's changed recently?" asked Mrs. Battles, the school psychologist.

"Yes, unfor...yes, it has. In early October, I started seeing a different Brendon. He seemed to come to school very unfocused and distracted every day... not doing much work, sort of lost in his own world, not really paying much attention during my lessons and during class discussions."

"Has the quality of his work been affected?" asked Mr. Larenzo, the school's special education teacher.

"Yes, it's been like night and day. He went from doing all of his work to doing almost no work. And the work he does do lately is usually done quickly, and not accurately. It's pretty obvious he just guesses to get finished with assignments as fast as he can. And lately, when I call on him, he often seems sort of startled, like I've woken him from a daydream or something. His answers to my questions during lessons are almost always inaccurate."

"In your opinion, could that be because the work is getting too difficult for him, or is it more a lack of effort and focus on his part?" asked Mr. Larenzo.

"I think it's a lack of effort and focus. Brendon's a smart boy, and he definitely has the skills to do the work. Definitely. And I'm also starting to see some disrespectful behavior from him, too. Like last week, right in the middle of a seatwork assignment, he got up, crinkled up his assignment paper and started walking toward the front of the room. I asked him to stop and return to his seat, but he totally ignored my request, walked to the front of the room and threw his paper into the trash can."

Mrs. Rollins looked surprised. "That doesn't sound like the Brendon I kn..."

"That's totally unacceptable behavior!" interrupted Mrs. Northgate, the school counsellor. "What were you thinking, Brendon, throwing your paper into the trash can? It's paper... that's gotta go in the recycling bin! You know, save our planet and everything!"

"I totally agree!" Mr. Larenzo chimed in. "Teaching children to be caretakers of the planet should be one of our top priorities! You should always use the recycling bin when you throw away your assignments! And I mean alwa..."

"Okay," interrupted Dr. Murdock, "let's steer back to the challenges we're seeing in the classroom. Are there any other concerns you haven't mentioned, Mrs. Patterson?"

"Yes, there's one more thing. I'm pretty sure Brendon has been cheating on some of his work lately, too. For example, on last week's spelling test one word was 'crayon', and he spelled it 'Crayola' on his test paper."

"That's totally awesome!" chuckled Mrs. Battles. "It's obvious Brendon peeked into his own desk to come up with that spelling. At least he was cheating creatively... not bad for a second grader!"

"Yeah, he didn't know the spelling," added Mrs. Northgate, "but he found a way to get the right answer. Well, almost the right answer. I think we don't spend enough time teaching problem-solving skills in the younger grades. Well done, Brendon!"

"I agree! Wouldn't it'a been funny if the word had been 'pencil', and he spelled it 'Ticonderoga'?" chuckled Mrs. Dawber, the school's behavior specialist.

"Well, now you're all just being silly," said Mrs. Rollins.

"Oh, speaking of silly," said Mrs. Squibner, the paraeducator who works in Mrs. Patterson's classroom. "The other day, 1st grader Josh

Myers was telling me about a Seahawk game he went to with his family this past weekend. He said one of the players got thrown out of the game, and as he walked off the field the crowd was booing him and, as Josh put it, he 'flip-flopped' the crowd."

"That is *too* funny!" laughed Mrs. Spanaway, the school's Title 1 teacher. "I was at that game... that player was pretty mad when he got thrown out. Flip-flopped the crowd... that is *too* funny!"

"Hey, do you know what the dinner plate said to his date?" asked Mrs. Northgate. "Dinner's on me!"

Everyone laughed hard at that one.

Mrs. Squibner jumped back in, "I've got one...do you know why birds fly south in the winter? Anyone? Because it's too far to walk!"

"Okay everyone," interjected Dr. Murdock, "we're getting close to being out of time here. We've heard a lot of very valuable information this morning... the results of informal academic testing from Mr. Larenzo and Mrs. Spanaway, observations of classroom and recess behavior from Mrs. Battles and Mrs. Northgate, and information from the home environment from you, Mrs. Rollins. Thank you, all of you. We have one more person to hear from, but first...Brendon, it's been great having you here with us this morning, but it's only 15 minutes until morning bell. Why don't you head over to the multi-purpose room and get some breakfast? We'll finish up with your mother while you're getting ready for your school day. Sound good?"

"Okay Dr. Murdock," he said as he grabbed his backpack. "Bye mom, have a great day!"

"You too, sweetie. Have an awesome day... see you at home," she said as she gave him a kiss on the forehead.

After the door closed, Dr. Murdock continued the discussion. "Natalie, we wanted to speak in private with you about the last piece of information we'll discuss today. Mrs. Battles?"

"Thank you, Dr. Murdock. I have the results of the psychological testing we received two days ago…testing done at the request of your former school district. It was done at the Woodland Mental Health Clinic at the end of last school year. The school psychologist at Brendon's former school sent it to me, with an apology that it took so long for them to forward these evaluation results to us. The findings go a long way toward explaining what we've been seeing with Brendon lately.

"There's a lot of information to discuss. But perhaps most importantly, the results show that Brendon has a frequent tendency to dis-associate from his own thoughts, and to assume the persona and perspective of others. The report says that this is evidence of a variation of a rare condition called Giovannini Mirror Syndrome. In a nutshell, a person with this syndrome imagines the environment they're in through the eyes of those around them, and mentally role-plays situations from their points of view. To a casual observer, it would just look like the person is daydreaming, like we've been seeing with Brendon in the classroom. I've shared these results with Dr. Murdock, and we agree that we have the expertise and resources here at our school to help Brendon with his unique challenges."

"The good news," said Dr. Murdock, "is that this condition can be somewhat controlled by medication, and by cognitive strategies we can teach Brendon. Now, as Mrs. Battles said, this is a rare condition, and the causes are unknown. It's believed to perhaps be caused by damage incurred when mother and fetus have incompatible blood types, or to the release of infectious substances in the placenta, or perhaps it's a genetic condition… they're just not sure. But in Brendon's case, I think it's important to ask ourselves… do you know how to make a Kleenex dance? Put a little boogie in it! I remember when I was a kid in school, I heard that joke one day at lunch, and I laughed so hard I had milk squirt out of my nose! Then there was this other time…"

THE PERILS OF PHYSICALLY RESTRAINING STUDENTS

It was late October in the North Cascadia School District. Don Snyder was one of the most experienced behavioral specialists in the district, and tomorrow he would be teaching a full-day training in the use of physical restraint techniques. Don had taught this training many times over the years, but his class would take on extra importance this year. The district had been experiencing an alarming number of violent behavior problems recently, and teachers and administrators were asking for more support from the district. Every school already had several staff members who were trained in verbally de-escalating behaviors, to try to keep situations from becoming violent. But sometimes such incidents ended up becoming violent, requiring the physical restraining of the student, and there were far fewer staff members who were trained and certified to put hands on students to restrain them. Tomorrow's training would certify twelve more teachers from across the district to perform this important and unpleasant task.

As Don sat reviewing his notes in his living room, he started drafting a mental outline of what he would say, and what he wished he could tell those teachers during the training. He would tell them that while these techniques serve a very important purpose, the physical restraining of any child is fraught with risk. First and foremost, there's the possibility of accidentally injuring the child, which is a gut-wrenching thought to even contemplate. You also, of course, risk injury to yourself. What Don wouldn't be telling those twelve teachers was that injuring a child while restraining them could possibly bring TV news crews to their school's doorstep. Or that injuring a child could damage, or even possibly end, their career.

Educational law states that staff are allowed to physically restrain a student only if the student poses a physical danger to others or to himself. Don used 'he' in his mental preparation, but of course any violent student could also be a 'she', which brings even deeper levels of concern when putting hands on them. Part of Don's lesson would include the 'when to restrain, and when not to restrain' decision tree, whose branches don't always make intuitive sense. For example, the destruction of property, even very expensive property, is *not* an acceptable reason to restrain students. Verbal de-escalation strategies would need to be used in those instances.

So, if a student was angrily walking through an empty classroom, picking up and then smashing every tablet in the room, staff would talk with the student to try to calm him down … since with an empty classroom, no one would be in danger. The school might lose a lot of valuable equipment, but staff would not be allowed to physically intervene. In this example, the responder would be well served to try to scoop up and rescue as many tablets as possible, even while talking with the student to de-escalate his behavior. Instances that do call for physical restraint, however, are a different matter entirely.

There was a time when violent behavior, extreme enough to require physical restraint, was a rarity in public schools. But when the law called the *Individuals with Disabilities Education Act* was passed, students with disabilities that had formerly been excluded from schools were integrated into mainstream classrooms...and rightfully so! It was a long-overdue and ethically-sound law that has been crucial to the educational development of millions of students with disabilities over the years. However, when those doors swung open, many students with significant emotional and/or behavioral problems, including very violent students, were also allowed inside.

Don had worked with many violent students over the years. It was his job, along with his special education team, to teach such students anger-management skills and strategies so they could become non-violent members of the school community and of society. Often, those students had only one strategy in their repertoires to use when they became angry, and that was to lash out violently toward the source of their anger. The months, and sometimes years, of lessons with these students were usually filled with violent pushback before they slowly learned to use non-violent anger-management strategies. Quite often over those months and years, those students needed to be restrained to keep them from injuring classmates, staff, or themselves.

There's an adage in the education industry that states: 'The only *100% safe* restraining technique is the one you never have to use'. This means two things: 1) the use of verbal de-escalation techniques is of paramount importance, and should always be used first, for extended lengths of time if necessary, to hopefully resolve situations and avoid the need to use physical restraint; and 2) when verbal intervention isn't successful, and restraining is necessary, the use of physical restraint techniques, even when properly utilized, could still possibly result in the physical injury of a child. This is true even when guidelines and steps are followed perfectly. Don pictured an example where an adrenaline-charged student who is being held by his arms could generate enough torque on his own...when writhing around trying to escape from restraint...to break or sprain his own arm or wrist, even if the restrainer is merely holding on without exerting any force of his own. Injuring a child would be terrible and unfortunate. The community's backlash, and the damage to the career of the staff member when news got out that he or she broke a kid's arm, would be terrible and unfortunate as well.

Don had done the research. He knew that several students had actually died while being restrained in American schools over the years. The biggest cause of those deaths had been asphyxiation, caused by the restrainer exerting extreme pressure onto the torso or neck of a student to pin him down. Teachers trained and certified in the use of approved techniques would never restrain students in that manner, or use any techniques that were not taught in the training. But there's this to consider: when a student's anger is starting to ramp up, often the staff member who responds is one trained to verbally de-escalate the situation. As stated earlier, most staff members trained to de-escalate situations are not also trained and certified in physical restraint.

What is that staff member to do if the verbal de-escalation doesn't work and the student explodes in anger and starts to punch and kick his classmates? That staff member has almost no choice but to jump to the aid of the students that are in danger, and most likely would have to pull the angry, violent student away and hold him in some fashion so that he doesn't hurt anyone. Suddenly an untrained, uncertified staff member is incorrectly restraining an out-of-control violent student.

Back when Don was just starting his career as a special education teacher, he had received some sage advice from a friend who was an experienced teacher in the district. That friend advised him to not take the restraint training... to not get certified in the use of restraint techniques. Taking the training, the friend had said, makes you the go-to person to respond to violent situations in your school. By not getting trained and certified, you can never be asked to restrain students, which could put your health or career in jeopardy. Don did go through the trainings, and now he himself taught those trainings. But sometimes, he wished he had heeded that advice.

Don often used real-life examples from his own teaching career when he taught this training. As a special education teacher for more than 15 years, he had plenty of examples to choose from. There was one specific incident he used in every training.

During his first year as a teacher, Don had been called upon to respond to an unsafe situation in a 6th grade classroom. The teacher had called the office for emergency help using her classroom phone. The principal was not in the building, so the office had called Don to ask him to respond. He had not yet received *any* de-escalation or restraint training at that point in his career. When he got to the classroom, he found the students all standing in one front corner of the room, with the teacher standing in front of them. In the back row, only one empty desk away from where Don stood in the doorway, was a boy who was clutching a pair of scissors, and repeatedly and violently stabbing the cover of his closed textbook. He only occasionally stopped doing that to instead scratch long furrows into the top of his desk. He was obviously very upset about something, and definitely presented a potential danger to his classmates and teacher. The teacher had done the correct thing by moving herself and the students as far away as possible from the angry boy.

And so, in this example, Don would ask his trainees... if they were the ones standing in that doorway, what would they do? Would this rise to the level of requiring restraining if verbal de-escalation was not successful? Should, perhaps, the police be called? After all, there was a weapon involved that could potentially injure the student, his classmates, the classroom teacher, or Don himself.

In the actual situation, he had tried to speak with the boy for several minutes to calm him down, but the boy seemed to be in some sort of angry trance, not looking up from his book-stabbing, and not responding to Don's words. Don made sure he stayed between the boy and the others in the classroom, in case the boy decided to charge toward them. He also made sure he was at least equally close to the door as the boy was, in case he decided to bolt. He knew he could not let him leave the room, not in that frame of mind, with scissors in hand.

What Don chose to do would not be found in any manual or taught in any training. He waited for an opportune moment, then lunged at the boy and grabbed the wrist of the hand that was holding the scissors. This escalated the boy's anger and adrenaline even more, and the boy tried very aggressively to pull his hand free, while using his other hand to hit and scratch Don. They wrestled for control of the scissors for several seconds, seconds that were frightening moments to Don. The student had a strong grip on the scissors, and Don would be in danger if the student wrestled his hand and the scissors free. He did eventually manage to pry the boy's fingers up, and get the scissors out of his hand. But then the boy became even angrier. Don backed off at that point, and let the boy run to the other side of the back of the room.

At that point, Don didn't pursue him... he let him retreat to that neutral corner, an area that was a good distance from both his classmates and the door. He instructed the teacher to calmly walk her students from the room.

When they were all safely out of the room, Don began what was to be a lengthy talk with the boy to bring him out of his angry mindset, and back to being able to rationally discuss what was bothering him. After more than twenty minutes, they were able to safely leave the room...to resume talks in the office, so that the classroom teacher could re-enter with her students.

This example always elicited robust conversation at trainings. The situation as it unfolded was a definite example of what *not* to do. The person Don had put most at risk was himself in that instance, but other than a few scratches, things did fortunately turn out just fine. He was lucky. His inexperience worked against him that day, and he soon learned that he should have exercised much more patience and used extended verbal de-escalation techniques (which he wasn't trained in yet) to guide that situation to a peaceful conclusion.

This example highlighted the need for staff to always make sure they consider their own safety, as well as the safety of others. It also pointed out the importance of new teachers receiving verbal de-escalation training before their teaching career even begins. Students don't wait weeks or months before exhibiting escalated behaviors, so teachers need to be trained and ready on day one. And Don had learned firsthand how dangerous it can be for an untrained teacher to try to resolve an escalating situation with an angry, violent student.

Don's various examples did indeed generate fruitful discussions. He followed the district's lesson plan for the training, as he always did. But he did not mention the possible career-threatening ramifications these teachers could face if they were to use the very techniques he was teaching them to use. He knew that the information and skills taught in this training would help keep students, staff, and visitors in the district's schools safe. That was the biggest fish to fry. But there was so much more information he wished he could have shared.

HUBCAPS AND WINE

Elisa White was one of the special education teachers at Crystal Ridge Middle School. She was only in her 4th year of teaching, but she had already seen a wide array of unexpected events they didn't prepare her for in college. She was about to add another item to that list.

Aside from being relatively young, Elisa was also a good-looking woman, so many of the boys in middle school had a big crush on her. In her mind, if that made any of them work extra hard to try to impress her, that was okay by her. She was always the model of professionalism, and careful not to let any students display any types of inappropriate behaviors.

Elisa was a Resource Room teacher, and most of her instruction was done in small groups that were 'pulled-out' to her room. Her 8th grade reading group had just sat down for their Tuesday morning lesson. The unit they were in had stories about various professions, and in today's story they were going to read about car mechanics. Teachers in her district were trained to start lessons by pre-emptively tapping into students' experiential knowledge of the main theme, to make sure they knew about the topic. If any students had no knowledge of the topic, this would serve as a primer to give them basic information prior to reading, so they had something to attach new learning to. If they did already have familiarity, this lead-in exercise was intended to activate their prior knowledge and make it 'sticky', so new learning would adhere more readily to what they already knew.

Elisa accomplished this for today's lesson by having each student in the small group talk about their own experience, or even their second-hand knowledge, of working on cars. One of the boys, Jared, talked about changing the spark plugs on his mom's car, and how he'd learned the hard way about making sure the spark plug wires were securely connected to the distributor cap. Sarah talked about how her dad wanted her to be able to change a flat tire, so she had practiced that with him in their driveway. Brian talked about how he and his dad would sometimes go to junkyards to find parts for an old car they were fixing up. David hadn't ever worked on cars, but he understood the basics of car engines, and now he knew that spark plug wires are connected to the distributor cap … thank you, Jared.

When the students finished talking, Elisa took a turn. She quipped that she had no knowledge of car engines, other than the location of her local car mechanic's shop. The students all laughed at her joke. She also said that she might need to do a junkyard visit herself someday, like Brian had mentioned, because she had lost one of the hubcaps off her 2006 Mustang. Brian told her he would keep his eyes open the next time he and his dad did their junkyard rounds. The two other boys in the group, not to be outdone, each said they would keep their eyes open as well. Brian responded by suggesting that he and his father had a better chance of locating just the right hubcap for that year and model of car. Jared scoffed at him, saying it would be easy to know which hubcap to look for by finding a picture of it online.

Elisa mentally rolled her eyes as she witnessed the teenage competitive pheromones at work. She had seen this happen before with these three boys, and was quick to re-direct them back to the story at hand.

It was her way of once again reminding them...if they wanted to earn brownie points with her, they could only do so by working hard during reading group each day. And they all did work hard that morning, as they pretty much always did.

It was a fairly uneventful Tuesday, and was shaping up to be an uneventful week. Toward the end of the day on Thursday, Elisa decided she needed some down time...a night out doing something fun. She checked with her friend Maggie, to see if she was free that night for dinner and perhaps a glass of wine or two. Maggie, who was a teacher at the district's high school, was on board with the idea.

They decided to meet at a local bistro, which happened to be inside the local shopping mall. Elisa knew this meant she might cross paths with students, or with parents of students, at the mall. But that was okay with her. There was a time at the beginning of her career when she was leery of letting local folks see her out for a night that involved drinking adult beverages, but she was over that at this stage of her career. Teachers are people too, and it wasn't like she was doing drugs or anything, so she was fine with the plans they'd made.

The mall was crowded that night, so she ended up having to park far away from the exterior entrance to the bistro. The closest entrance to where she parked was the main entrance to the mall, which would mean she'd have to walk partway through the mall to get to the bistro. She knew making that choice would increase her chances of seeing familiar faces. She opted for using the exterior entrance to the bistro, even though it was a slightly longer walk for her. She smiled to herself as she walked that extra distance, thinking that she apparently wasn't totally comfortable yet with the idea of seeing students or parents during a night out on the town.

She and Maggie had been first-year teachers together in the district, and had met at the district's 'new teacher orientation' trainings four years earlier. They had hit it off right away, and hung out together a lot over those three days of trainings. They'd formed a strong friendship since then, always having lots of things in common to talk about. Maggie was also a pretty young lady, so they even had stories to share about dealing with teenage boys, and sometimes, the fathers of their students.

At the bistro that evening, Maggie talked about a certain father (without mentioning his name, because she too was always very professional) that had signed up to be a volunteer in her classroom. This man tended to gawk at Maggie to a degree that often made her uncomfortable, and sometimes said things that were a tad awkward. She had a feeling he'd signed up to be a helper because he wanted to be around Maggie, and not so much to help students. She asked Elisa for advice, which she was happy to give.

Elisa had been through a similar situation two years earlier, and things had gotten so uncomfortable that she had ended up asking her principal to talk with that father. That, in turn, had also made her uncomfortable. The father immediately stopped volunteering in her classroom, and didn't attend conferences for the rest of that year. Even to this day, Elisa wasn't sure she had done the right thing. But she did make the 'talk to your principal' suggestion to Maggie, along with the pros and cons of taking that action.

To lighten the conversation a bit, Elisa brought up the pheromone competition incident from her reading group earlier in the week, and they both chuckled at that all-too-familiar occurrence. Maggie could relate; as a high school teacher, she was used to being around lots of hormone-driven teenage boys. Both ladies agreed that working at an elementary school would be *so* much easier, at least as far as *students'* crushes were concerned.

Elisa ended up staying out a bit later than she had planned, but it was great seeing Maggie and catching up on things with her friend. Besides, she had really needed the recreational mental break. So even with less sleep, she woke up quite refreshed the next morning. She actually left for work earlier than normal, driving to her school in the dark for the first time in a while. But even that didn't affect her mood... she felt very happy and centered following her fun night out. And, it was Friday!

She enjoyed having the extra time to settle into her day, and she smiled as she happily poured herself into her lesson prep for her morning groups. About five minutes before the morning bell, her student Brian walked into her classroom. After they exchanged greetings, Brian smiled, hesitated a moment for effect, and proudly pulled a used hubcap out of his backpack and handed it to Elisa. He said he was totally sure it was the right size and style for her 2006 Mustang. Elisa was pleasantly surprised, and thanked Brian. She wasn't expecting any of the boys to actually follow through on finding her a hubcap, especially so soon. She asked how much it cost, so she could reimburse him. But Brian said it was 'no charge', because the owner of the junkyard had not charged him for it. Elisa smiled at that news, and thanked him again for his kindness and effort, and gratefully took the hubcap. Brian was obviously pleased he could do something nice for her, and walked out wearing a big smile.

At the end of the day, Elisa placed the hubcap in a paper bag, not really sure she should have accepted such a favor from one of her students, and walked to the staff parking lot a bit sheepishly. She hoped no one would ask her what was in the bag, and no one did. When she got to her car, she put the bag on the roof and got her keys out. As she unlocked the door, she noticed something that made her stop short, smile, and shake her head in disbelief. One of her other hubcaps was missing.

THE SCARY TRANSITION
TO MIDDLE SCHOOL

It happened during a science lesson in early May. Billy had already been eagerly looking forward to the autumn, when he and his classmates would be entering that almost-mythical destination...middle school. It loomed on the horizon like a beckoning pre-teen utopia, and he couldn't wait to get there. And today's lesson on a butterfly's life cycle helped Billy put it all into perspective. Peterman Elementary had been a cocoon, preparing him for a re-birth into the new world of middle school... with the warm spring weather providing the perfect backdrop to his metamorphosis.

But when the calendar flipped to June, something changed. He found that his excitement was beginning to morph into a bubbling stew of mild panic, apprehension, and self-doubt. Billy was the youngest of three kids in his family, and he had heard many stories of the new opportunities that would soon be opening up for him at Vandelay Middle School. But when he thought about those stories the past few days, the only butterflies to be found were the ones fluttering around in his stomach.

Billy didn't know it, but his parents were even more nervous than he was about the upcoming transition. They had spent some sleep-deprived nights worrying about what September might bring. Billy was a special education student, with fairly significant social/emotional challenges. He was naive, immature, and emotionally fragile, with under-developed social skills. On top of all that, his birth date made him one of the youngest and smallest kids in his grade level. So, when it came right down to it, his parents were concerned that he might not be ready to enter the uncharted waters of middle school.

They requested a meeting with his special education teacher, Mrs. Ross, to discuss the possibility, and the wisdom, of requesting that Billy perhaps be retained in 5th grade for one more year.

"Hello and welcome," said Mrs. Ross, as Mr. and Mrs. Humphrey walked into the Resource Room. "It's great to see you both again."

"Nice to see you again too," said Mrs. Humphrey. "We look forward to this discussion."

"Nice to see you again, Mrs. Ross," said Mr. Humphrey. "Thank you for making time for us. I'm sure you have more important things to do than meet with worried parents whose kid is about to go into junior high."

"Middle school," said Mrs. Humphrey.

"I'm happy to make time for this," she replied. "This can be a nervous time for parents…their kid going from a comfortable, secure elementary school into the scary unknowns of middle school. You'd be surprised how many parents either call me or request meetings to discuss this very topic. So, no worries, I'm happy to help in any way I can. It's good that you arranged to come without Billy being here…it'll allow us to speak more openly about concerns."

After they took their seats, Mrs. Ross continued, "You know, one of the things I love most about being a special education teacher is that I often get to work with kids for many years, and get to know their parents for many years as well. I've been working with Billy since the beginning of 2nd grade, so I've had the privilege of knowing the three of you for almost four years now. It will now also be my privilege to help you smooth this transition into middle school."

"We appreciate that, Mrs. Ross," replied Mrs. Humphrey. "And we appreciate everything you and your team have done for Billy, and for us, over those years."

"It's been our pleasure," she said. "Tell you what, since Billy's not here…feel free to call me Elaine if you'd like. I'd say we know each other well enough now."

"Sounds good, Elaine…and you can call us Helen and Frank," said Helen.

"Okay, thank you. So, how can I help you, Helen and Frank?" she said with a smile.

"Well," said Helen, "we're concerned about Billy going into middle school, and so we're not really sure what to do."

"And we would really value your input about this decision," said Frank. "We feel that you know Billy as well as we do, and maybe even better…when it comes to sensing how ready he is to make this big step. What advice can you give us?"

"This type of situation has so many moving parts," Elaine replied. "There isn't an exact science that goes into decisions like these. I can tell you what the research says, and I can give you my opinions. Academically, Billy is totally ready to be successful in 6th grade. And that's a very important thing to keep in mind as we talk about other areas of readiness. With that said, there are several things you should consider as you weigh this decision.

"Research tells us that retention, especially after the primary grades, can have many significant negative effects on a student. First of all, there's the stigma of being 'the kid who got held back'. Next year, if he was in 5th grade again, all the new kids in 5th grade would know he'd been held back. And while Billy's self-concept has become somewhat stronger over these past few years, we all know he's still got a fragile and impressionable personality. He cares deeply about how others view him. Some, or even many 5th graders next year might see him as somewhat of an outlander, and he might feel the same way about himself.

"Also, if he was retained, he'd be starting next year with most of his friends gone from the school, and many of those kids are, to a large extent, his support group. Most of his classmates have been with Billy for years now, and they've sort of taken him under their wing and looked after him...they're very much invested in making sure he's okay. So, him going into middle school in September with his supporting cast of friends would be a strong reason for him to promote to 6th grade."

"Those are very good points, and nice to hear," said Frank. "Please, continue."

"And keep in mind," Elaine said, "the potential stigma concerns could also spill over into your neighborhood, and his friends there. We've worked hard on friendship skills in our social skills group...how to make and keep friends, but it would be very hard for him if those friends started to treat him differently, or if they said mean things. They might just poke a little fun at him about being held back, and he might misconstrue that as a major criticism."

"Another good point," replied Helen.

"So okay," said Elaine, "now let's look more closely at Billy being very strong academically. I'd be very concerned that repeating the 5th grade curriculum would, frankly, be boring to him; that it would be way too easy for him. And don't lose sight of this either...right now Billy has a great work ethic. He always works very hard, and wants to please all of us with his work ethic and his great grades. If he repeated 5th grade, I'd be concerned he'd learn to coast along without having to work hard, and that his work ethic could be affected on a long-term basis."

"We had thought of the part where he might get bored," said Frank, "but not that part about work ethic."

"Yes, we thought that maybe his 5th grade teacher next year could adapt his curriculum so it could be more challenging," said Helen. "But that's a great point you make about work ethic. His work ethic makes us very proud."

"And speaking of being proud," said Elaine, "holding him back would probably send an unintentional message that all of his hard work this year wasn't enough, that he wasn't successful enough to earn a promotion to 6th grade. Even if you told him otherwise. He would want to know why he's being held back, and there's not an easy way to explain that. And then also, maybe he'd think you weren't proud of him for what he'd accomplished. That might, in turn, devastate him and negatively impact his motivation and self-concept. Again, there are a lot of moving parts that are inter-linked here. A lot of his self-worth is wrapped up in his excellent academic successes."

"Wow, so many things we didn't think of," said Helen. "Thank you so much for sharing. Anything else on the 'don't retain' side of this?"

"Yes," Elaine replied, "there's this to consider. Billy has never been a behavior problem…not ever. But if he was retained, suddenly we'd have a somewhat bored student sitting in a classroom with much less mature students than he's used to being around, especially the boys. Some boys at the beginning of 5th grade are still in the class-clown, immature stage, and tend to act out immaturely to get attention. Things like making fart noises to get giggles, shooting spitballs, giggling loudly when other kids make fart noises, you know, that kind of interplay. So, if he was retained, he'd be going from having positive, mature role-models in his classroom, to having much more immature social modeling from male classmates."

"One more thing for us to think about," said Helen. "Boy, we have quite a list of reasons not to retain. Any others to add?"

"Those are the major ones I wanted to bring up," said Elaine. "Let's jump to the other side of the ledger…reasons why it could possibly be a positive thing for Billy to repeat 5th grade. Certainly, staying one more year at this school would provide stability and familiarity. He knows the building, the routines, the teachers, the schedules. And, he does have a few friends in the 4th grade, next year's 5th grade, that he plays with at recess, and that he's been in special ed groups with. So, he would have *some* friends already in place at this school next year. Oh, and he also of course knows me, and my special ed staff…he's very comfortable with us."

"Oh, he just loves you and your staff!" replied Helen. "Being with you guys again would be a huge check mark in the plus column. That would be a great comfort to us as parents, too."

"That's nice of you to say," Elaine replied. "I know that Billy knows we care about him a great deal, and that we would always do whatever we can to help him in every regard."

"I have to say," said Frank, "like Helen just said…him having another year with you and your staff would be a huge positive for him, and for us."

"I appreciate that, very much," said Elaine. "Now, we should all keep in mind that while the comfort and security of returning to this school, and of being with my staff and me again is something to consider, the other side of that coin is perhaps even more important for him. I'm talking about the growth involved with him letting go of that security, and learning to thrive in a new environment with new staff. And, of course, that new staff would also care a great deal about him."

"Actually," said Helen, "it might be harder for Frank and me to let go of the security of Peterman than it would be for Billy."

"I think you're right, sweetie," said Frank.

"As you know, Elaine," Helen said, "we have two older kids who've gone to Vandelay. With our oldest, Susan, there were no problems at all. She's always been very mature for her age, and she handled the transition with flying colors. Her brother Drake wasn't quite as mature as his sister, but he also had no problems for the most part. When he got into 7th and

8th grade, he did make some bad choices of people to hang out with, and we learned that he started smoking pot when he was with those friends. But he's always had a good head on his shoulders, never one to be pushed into doing something he didn't want to do. So, he was okay in middle school. We wish he was still there this coming year, so he could look out for his little brother. But we missed out on that by one year…he'll be going into high school this year. So, we have a lot of transitions going on in our family!"

"You really do!" said Elaine.

"Now, the experiences with Drake turned out okay," Helen continued, "but they did open our eyes to the kinds of pitfalls that students in middle school can face. We're just not sure that Billy has that same 'good head on his shoulders' that his brother has. We're concerned that he'll be easily led into doing things he shouldn't do."

"Or that he'll become an easy target for older kids to pick on or bully… you know how kind kids can be at that age," Frank said, sarcastically.

"So, let's talk about that," Elaine replied. "The potential negatives at Vandelay that would be of concern. I want you to keep in mind that for every concern I'm about to bring up, we'll have a plan drafted, specially-tailored to Billy's needs, that'll be put into place to alleviate the concerns. That's part of my job…those strategies will be built-into his special ed transition plan that I'll write.

"Our district has an excellent outline of steps that get taken," she added. "We elementary special ed teachers work with staff from Vandelay to develop plans to make each student's transition successful. I'll meet with the middle school staff early next week, and we'll develop that plan for Billy. I'll email the plan to you when it's finalized at our end, so you can take a look and give any input you'd like to suggest that we include."

"We'll look forward to reading that," said Frank. "And we'll get back to you right away."

"That'll be great," Elaine replied. "Okay, let's look now at concerns, and address them one by one. First, the questions of him being naive and immature, with social skills that are…still developing. His special ed program will of course continue in 6th grade; he'll still be in pull-out groups with other students to work on shoring up each of those areas of concern. His resource room teacher next year, Mr. Newman, is an excellent teacher, with an excellent reputation of working well with kids with social skills issues. And, and this is not just a little thing, I feel it would be great for Billy to have one more solid male role-model in his life at school. My staff and I care about Billy, but we're all women, so that change would be a big plus for Billy. And Vandelay uses the same social skills curriculum we use here at Peterman, so the lessons would pick right up where we leave off. And Billy has done great within this curriculum. So, any questions so far about any of that?"

"We've only had good experiences with the staff at Vandelay," said Helen. "But of course, we haven't had dealings with the special education staff over there. It's good to hear that they have such a good reputation."

"They really do," said Elaine. "Billy would be in very good hands. Now, he'll have other teachers, other than Mr. Newman, of course. But it will be Mr. Newman's responsibility to make sure Billy's teachers all become familiar with his educational plan. Before the school year starts, he'll meet with each of Billy's teachers, and go over his transition plan and his IEP. Those documents will spell out all of the accommodations and modifications that Billy requires. Those teachers, and Mr. Newman, would still be working off of the IEP and transition plan that I wrote, so his entire program would look the same over at Vandelay. But they would include some new accommodations that I'll suggest, like seating him near some friends from Peterman in the classroom who would be supportive.

"They'll also give Billy some extra opportunities to become oriented to the building and campus. We'll choose a few responsible Peterman alums that will be going into 7th grade, and they'll take Billy under their wings and look out for him. During the first several weeks, they can help him navigate his way around, show him where everything is, help him with his schedule, and so on. And we'll assign a 6th grade counsellor to mentor Billy, someone he can always turn to if he needs to talk about anything at all.

"And as you know, I'll be taking all my 5th grade special ed kids on a field trip over to Vandelay next week to walk them around and give them an orientation tour. They'll get a chance to meet Mr. Newman, and some other staff. We won't know who Billy's homeroom classroom teacher will be until probably July, so he can't meet him or her yet. But there *will* be a 'back to school' night in late August, where you'll be able to bring Billy in to meet his new teacher. I know you've probably been to those before, with Susan and Drake?"

"We've been to a bunch of those," said Frank. "It's always a very welcoming event…very professionally done."

"Vandelay has a terrific staff," said Elaine. "When school starts, they'll be very thorough in acclimating all of the incoming 6th graders. Over the first few weeks, they'll make sure everybody knows what's what…they'll go over all the rules and information the kids will need to know. And I'll go over the Vandelay Student Handbook with Billy and the other special ed students these next few weeks…we'll read all of the rules and expectations they'll need to know about, and new opportunities they can look forward to as Vandelay Wildcats. I'm sure Billy will read the handbook over and over, so he knows what to expect.

"There are, of course, a lot of new perks and opportunities for him to look forward to in middle school, like sports and band and school dances. And, if I know Billy, he'll get excited about the huge amount of choices for lunches every day!"

"That boy loves to eat…there's no doubt he'll love the variety of pizza, burgers, and so on," said Frank. "That's something Drake has been telling him about, and Billy's excited about that."

"Now, let's discuss the concept of protecting Billy from upper classmen who might be bad influences," Elaine said. "You already know that Vandelay is pretty much segregated into 6th, 7th and 8th grade pods. There are very few times during a day when 6th graders even cross paths with 7th or 8th grade kids. Before and after school are the prime times they might meet up. And those are times that we can lean on mentors and supportive peers to keep a watchful eye. We can't insulate him at all times, and actually, I don't think we'd want to do that. I get the feeling that Billy has a better head on his shoulders than you might think. And this would be a great opportunity for him to grow in that regard. We can let him know that we'll be trusting him to make good decisions...that we know he'll always do what he knows is right, and that we trust him to do so. That we *expect* him to do so.

"Which is a great segue into one more important concept to consider... such a very important concept in life...*expectations*. If a kid feels that his parents and teachers have low expectations for him, he might just lower his own expectations for himself. So, this is your chance to set *all* of your expectations high. Billy has a lot of self-pride in everything he does, and I know he'll want to make you proud in every way he can next year, like he's done here at Peterman."

"He is, and he should be, very proud of all he's accomplished here at Peterman," said Helen. "And we are so very proud of him. Those plans all sound great, Elaine. It's comforting to hear that so much goes into helping kids make the big transition successfully...all of the behind-the-scenes work that parents don't get to hear about. I guess unless they get nervous and ask for a meeting, like we did."

"I'm glad this has helped. I think you can see that the few reasons to consider retention are overwhelmed by the many reasons you should let Billy promote to 6th grade. I know it's hard, so I'm glad you requested this meeting. Hopefully, now you can feel better about, and actually enjoy, what is about to be a proud, wonderful milestone for Billy, and for both of you. It will be a happy, proud time for your whole family."

Helen started to tear up. "We can see now that it's time for us to let go and let him fly from the nest, so to speak. Peterman has been such a great nest, and you've been such a wonderful mother bird to him, Elaine. Thank you, so much...for everything. Having this discussion with you has helped us more than you'll ever know."

On the evening of August 28th, Helen, Frank, and Billy walked through the front doors of Vandelay Middle School. It was indeed a milestone moment for them, and they were all three very proud that they were, in their own ways, ready for this new beginning.

AN ALARMING
MANIFESTATION

A family moved into the catchment area of one of the elementary schools in our district last spring...but as it turned out, that school was already at their cap limit for students. Our school was selected to take their overflow enrollments, so I was about to add that family's son to my special education caseload. Of the hundreds of special ed students I'd known over the course of my career, Ian's confidential records indicated that he just might turn out to be the most violent and dangerous student I would ever work with.

When I received his files, a few days before he was going to enroll at our school, I couldn't believe what I was reading. Ian's track record of violence and destructive behavior was remarkable to me...and I had worked with dozens of extremely violent students over my two and a half decades of teaching special education. On paper, Ian had them all beat, and the information in his files made me question the wisdom of even letting him attend our school.

I've always been very much in favor of allowing all special education students into public schools, and this was the first time I had ever balked at welcoming a special needs student into our own mainstream school environment. I certainly wasn't shying away from taking on the challenge of working with this youngster, but his history of violence was alarming. If I was the parent of a student in his assigned 5th grade classroom, knowing what his file said about his behavioral history, there would be no way I'd allow my child to be in that classroom.

The red flags in his files caused me to seek out my principal, to discuss the possibility of looking into switching Ian's placement to a more appropriate option within our district's cascade of services. She and I went over all the details in his records, and she completely agreed with me. There were self-contained special education classrooms in our district that were specifically designed and staffed to work with students like Ian. Kids that were too violent to be in mainstream classrooms were instead placed in these classrooms to work on anger-management strategies and other behavioral skills. There was a strong ratio of adults to students in these rooms, and a curriculum that targeted the unique, specific needs of violent students.

Despite our significant concerns and our feelings that Ian would be better served in one of these behavioral self-contained rooms, our hands, and the district's hands, were tied by special education law. Ian would indeed need to be placed at our school, because his existing IEP (Individualized Education Program), written by his former district, stipulated that he should be placed in a mainstream classroom with 'pull-out' special education assistance. Because his IEP inexplicably called for mainstream placement, that's where he would need to be placed. If we wanted to see him eventually placed in a self-contained behavioral classroom, he would first need to go through a complete Special Education re-evaluation. Normally, special education students get re-evaluated every three years, and Ian's next due date wouldn't be for another eighteen months. We could request an early re-evaluation, but it would take a few months before that process could even begin.

So, it looked like we were going to have to make this work at our school. All of our schedules, mine and those of my paraeducators, were already maxed out…every minute of our days were already assigned across the thirty-plus existing students on our caseload. It was very common to have new students arrive throughout the year, and for me to need to re-work a few peoples' schedules to accommodate those new arrivals. But Ian was going to require an inordinate amount of change to everyone's schedule; he would require extensive service time (essentially, someone with him at all times) if we were going to ensure the safety of his peers and staff, and give him the type of instruction and supervision he needed. If (when) he displayed violent behaviors, we would need to keep specific data records of those behaviors over the next few months before we could: 1) make a request for an early re-evaluation process to begin, and 2) begin to make recommendations that he be served in one of the self-contained behavioral placement options in our district.

It boiled down to this: we couldn't pre-emptively place him in a safer, more appropriate environment; we had to allow him the chances to repeatedly demonstrate the violent behaviors we already knew he would exhibit. It was our job during those months to keep records of how many injuries he would inflict, and then use that data to make our case for the eventual more appropriate and beneficial self-contained classroom placement.

Ian's mother had indicated that he would begin attending our school in three days, so I had to develop an in-school plan and adjust everyone's schedules very quickly. It's standard practice to call the special education teacher of a student's previous school to gather information about what might have worked for them, and to perhaps incorporate any strategies they found useful and effective into the plan I'd be developing.

I'll never forget how that teacher reacted when I told her I was going to be Ian's new special ed teacher. She told me that my life was about to change, in a *very* bad way…those were the first words out of her mouth!

She said she had never worked with any student that was even remotely as violent as Ian, and that she fully expected that he would end up being arrested and in juvenile detention before he became a teenager. After she shared some data and potential strategies that had occasionally worked for them, she told me she felt sorry for me…and wished me good luck.

After we talked, and after re-reading all of his files, I had a fairly clear picture of the student that would be arriving in a few days. It was going to be a challenge for sure, and we needed to be ready from the very first minute he walked through our doors.

There's a relevant special education law (and process), called Manifestation Determination, that would significantly impact the strategies we would be allowed to use with Ian. He was eligible for special education services as a student with an emotional/behavioral disability, and his violent behavior had been deemed to be a 'manifestation of his disability' by his previous district…meaning that it was his disability that was causing him to exhibit violent behaviors. Normally, a student who violently attacks and injures others at school would get suspended (or even expelled, if the attack was violent enough) from school, partly as a negative consequence to the behavior, and partly to help keep the school safe.

However, this law says that since his violent behavior was caused by his disability, Ian couldn't be 'punished' via suspension for hurting others…because violent behavior was beyond his control and not really his fault. In the eyes of the law, it's up to the special education program to 'teach' the violence out of a student's repertoire of behaviors. So, instead of suspending a kid like Ian when he hurt others, the school/district would be required to modify his special education plan to make it more effective, while also doing whatever it took to keep other kids and staff safe.

The law doesn't give violent students a complete pass; students who exhibit violent behavior (even when the behavior is determined to be a manifestation of their disability) *can* be suspended, but only for a total of ten days in a school year. Because students are aware of this ten-day limit, it can give them a sense of impunity with regard to their actions as they approach or reach that total, which creates a significant disadvantage for staff members who work with them.

Actually, I agree with the premise of this law. It's a beneficial facet of the *Individuals with Disabilities Education Act* that really does help protect the rights of students with behavioral disabilities. But there are times that it also doesn't allow schools to use their full repertoire of strategies and interventions to do the difficult work of training violent students to use non-violent strategies when they get angry.

There had been a few times in my career when we'd received advanced copies of files of soon-to-be-new students that painted a challenging picture of their behaviors, only to find that the kid wasn't anywhere near as challenging as the files had led us to believe. Sometimes, moving to a new school can give a student a chance to get off to a positive start, gain positive momentum (which can be reinforced in a number of positive ways) and leave their challenges behind them for the most part. There was a chance, in other words, that Ian might embrace this new opportunity and hit the ground running in a mostly-positive, non-violent fashion.

We teach all students that bad choices they make don't have to ruin the rest of their day; such choices can be learned from, and worked past in a positive manner. In a similar, but more global manner of thinking, we would be letting Ian know that his past transgressions would not be held against him. It was important from the get-go that he understood (and believed) that his new school, and teachers, would give him a fresh start and a chance to hit 'reset' with a blank slate. That was going to be our welcoming, positive message to Ian and his mother.

His mainstream classroom teacher was carefully chosen, and she, our principal, my team and I had two lengthy after-school meetings to put Ian's educational plan into place. Our district's Special Education Assistant Director and I worked to develop the type of data-recording system we would use from day one to keep track of Ian's behaviors. We put together a reinforcement plan that would encourage and reward positive behaviors and interactions, and a response plan that would be used if verbal de-escalation of behaviors was needed, or if it turned out that physical restraint would be necessary. I was one of only two staff members who were trained and certified to physically restrain students, so a rotation system was established in case it was necessary for either of us to leave our group sessions to verbally de-escalate his behavior, or to restrain him if his behavior became violent.

Most importantly, we prepared ourselves to welcome Ian with a unified message and vibe of high expectations and positive new beginnings. We felt as prepared as we could feel, considering the short turn-around time we were given to make our plans for his arrival. We were determined to make his experience at our school positive, beneficial, and safe for everyone involved.

As it turned out, Ian never attended our school. The day before he was supposed to start, his (divorced) parents agreed that he should go live with his father in Idaho instead of with his mother in our town in Washington state. Apparently, they determined that the father was better prepared to give him the type of home life he needed in order to be successful. I was surprised when I heard that news, but I can't say that I was disappointed. We had spent a lot of time developing our plans and altering our schedules to accommodate Ian's expected behaviors, and we were ready to welcome him and give him the best of our efforts. But frankly, we all felt pretty relieved that we wouldn't be having to deal with his violent behaviors. I hoped that Ian was going to be successful in his new school in Idaho. I passed along his records and my positive best wishes to his new special education teacher.

TEACHING ADDITION
TO YOUNGSTERS

Hi Madeline,

It was nice talking with you on the phone earlier today. During this Covid-19 remote-learning era, it will be important for us to communicate on an ongoing basis, so that you'll always know the best strategies to use with Kenzie at home to augment her online learning. Since she only qualifies for special ed assistance in math, you'll be working (as you know) with her mainstream classroom teacher with regard to other academic subjects. I'll give you a summary here of what I'd suggest you work on this week in math, along with the strategies I'd recommend that you use. By the way, as we work together during the 'online learning' portion of the school year, consider me to be your on-going teammate...I'll let you know what specific skills to work on with Kenzie, and I'll make further recommendations as we move on to other math skills.

The following lesson walks Kenzie through the very first steps of learning to add. It will also help her conceptualize what addition is...what it's used for, and how it's used in real-life situations. You'll notice that the lesson I'm sending in this email breaks the process down in a step-by-step fashion, targeting very specific sub-skills and strategies. By using these steps when you practice with her at home, it will really bolster what we teach her online. And because you'll be using the exact strategies we'll use, and the same terminology, it will make our teamwork very effective.

Kenzie already knows how to count very well, and we'll be making good use of her strong counting skills in the strategies we work on. It's awesome that counting is a sub-skill she's already good at, so that's something to celebrate…but we need to improve her *use* of counting in one specific way. Here's what I mean, and what we need to work on:

I'm going to first show you the *eventual* strategy she'll use, so you can see what we're targeting as our goal. Then later in this email, I'll walk you through the prerequisite skill lesson that must be taught first. So, if the problem, for example, is '8 plus 6', the process will eventually be done this way:

1. Make sure 8 + 6 is prominently written on a paper in front of her, and read it out loud to her; then walk her through these next steps…

2. Tell her that 8 + 6 means you start with eight things, and then you get 6 more…so then we need to find out how many *total* things we now have *altogether*.

3. She would start by locking the number 8 into her head (I have kids touch their forehead and say 'I lock 8 in my head'), and then she would say out loud '8, 8, 8, 8'…so she can remember that she's already locked in the number 8.

4. She then puts up 6 fingers.

5. Knowing that 8 is already locked in her head, she would start counting up from there, one number for each finger she's holding up (so, '9, 10, 11, 12, 13, 14'). We'd make sure she starts with 9…she needs to remember that 8 is already locked in her head, so she'll need to start with the number

that comes *after* 8; that specific concept should get worked on carefully each time you do an addition problem.

Before you do the process described above with her, you first need to do the process described below several times over several days' lessons. You'll be using manipulatives to help her grasp the concept (and process) of addition in a concrete manner. You already have a bag of manipulatives (counting tiles ... colorful little plastic squares) that we use for this activity; they were part of the Resource Room math packet you picked up earlier this week.

You should use the tiles as follows ... I'll use the same '8 plus 6' as an example:

1. Prominently display 8 + 6 and read it out loud.
2. Tell her that 8 + 6 means you start with eight things, and then you get 6 more ... so then we need to find out how many *total* things we now have *altogether*.
3. Make a line of 8 red (or whatever color) blocks. Ask her to tell you how many blocks are in that line, she'll count them, probably silently, and tell you that there's 8. You should say 'Oh yeah? Prove it to me!' She'll count them out loud for you and prove there's 8.
4. Near that line, put a second line of 6 blocks of another color (tell her there's 6 blocks in that line, you should count those out loud for her, to prove to her that there's 6).
5. Read the problem out loud again. Point to the red blocks and say, "We're going to start with 8 blocks, then we get 6 more (point to line of 6), so now we need to find out how many *total* blocks we now have *altogether*."
6. Ask her again, "Remind me, how many red blocks were

there?" (You'll see why that's important in a moment...when she says 8, ask her to prove it again).

7. Now say 8 + 6 again out loud and tell her that now she'll need to find out how many *red and blue* blocks there are *altogether*. Tell her she'll find that out by counting how many total blocks there are. She should go ahead and do that now, starting with the red blocks. So, she'll go: 1, 2, 3, 4, 5, 6, 7, 8, then she'll look to the blue blocks and continue: 9, 10, 11, 12, 13, 14. Pardon me for being so overly-descriptive there, but there's a reason. Have her do that same thing one more time.

8. Tell her she's going to do that same thing again, but this time she doesn't need to do that 1, 2, 3, 4, 5, 6, 7, 8 part...she *already knows* there's 8 blocks in that line...she proved it to you a bunch of times. So, she should simply touch the red line and say '8', then look to the blue line to continue counting, starting with 9 and going to 14. This is a concrete visual demonstration of what she'll eventually be doing without the blocks.

9. One of the most important parts is the step where she no longer has to count up the original line of 8, that she can simply start with that number already established (locked) in her mind, then continue counting with the next number as she 'adds' on that new amount to the original amount to find the *total* number of blocks.

10. You can choose any addition problems that use two single-digit numbers to work on this strategy. Eventually, we'll start making one of the numbers a double-digit 'teen' number, but she's not ready for that yet. Also, eventually we'll work on having her pick out the bigger of the two single-digit numbers in the problem and have her use that one as the one that she starts with...the one that gets locked into her head. That not only makes the problem easier, but since she'll need to

put up fingers for the second number, it's a way to ensure that she always has enough fingers to use for this strategy when we move into adding one single-digit and one double-digit number.

One more little, but important, thing. Right now, if we ask her to put up, say, nine fingers, she's still at the stage where she needs to count her fingers one at a time to make sure she has 9 fingers held up. There are two things you can work on at home to help her get more efficient at that. We've already started to work on both of these strategies, but she needs more repetitions.

First, start with numbers 5 or less. Tell her to put up 5 fingers (she already has learned this one with us…that putting up 5 fingers means putting up all the fingers on one hand)…so she should be able to put up 5 fingers automatically, without having to count them. She can also put up 2, and of course 1 finger without having to count them. But she needs to get better at 3 and 4. So have a fun 'flash quiz' game with her from time to time: "Ready? Put up 3 fingers, oh yeah? 5 fingers, 2 fingers, 4, 1, etc." Our aim here is for her to never have to count any of those amounts of fingers for the numbers 5 and less. She's right on the verge of already having this mastered.

The second one is a bit trickier, but she'll totally be able to do this soon. And this skill is very related, as you'll see, to our addition processes described above. Tell her, "Put up 7 fingers." She'll probably default to counting '1, 2, 3, 4, 5' on one hand, and then continuing '6, 7' using the other hand. Our goal here is to get her to put up all 5 fingers at once on the first hand and say "5"…then look at the other hand and count "6, 7." She'll need more repetitions and reminders that she doesn't need to count "1, 2, 3, 4, 5" for that first hand, and that's a skill we'll work toward solidifying with her.

So anyway, those are the specific strategies I'd suggest you work on with her at home when you're practicing addition this week. As we move on to more advanced addition, or to other math skills, I'll email again with lesson updates and strategies for you to use. Let me know if you have any questions ... or how I can be of any further help.

Take care and stay healthy!
Mr. H

THE POETRY SESSIONS

SESSION ONE

"Raise your hand if you've ever been out hiking or walking around, and suddenly you saw something beautiful or amazing...like a rainbow, or a field of flowers, or a great view of Mount Rainier, and the first thing you did was grab your phone to take a bunch of pictures."

Mr. L didn't have to wait long for a response. All of the students immediately raised their hands.

"Okay," he continued, "tell me why you did that; why would you take pictures of that beautiful or amazing thing you saw? Thanks for raising your hand...Megan?"

"Because, if it's beautiful, I'd want to be able to share it with other people," she answered. "Like show it to my mother or my friends when I got home, so they could enjoy the beautiful sight, too."

"Great answer, Megan!" he replied. "I like the way you thought right away about sharing the beautiful image with others, so they could enjoy it, too. Certainly, wanting to share the wonderful moment would be one big reason for taking pics with your phone. Any other reasons you would take photos? Keeshana?"

"Because maybe I, myself, would want to re-visit what I saw at a later time. If it made me happy when I saw it, I think it would also make me happy every time I looked at a picture of it. It would remind me of the moment, like a nice souvenir...a lovely memory."

"Another excellent answer," said Mr. L. "I really like your word 'souvenir'. I agree that the photos would be exactly that. People buy souvenirs when they travel so they can kind of re-visit a place or re-live an experience over and over again after they come home. Excellent thinking. Any other reasons?" No one raised their hand, so he continued.

"Okay, those were the two reasons I wanted to discuss, so great job of thinking of those, Megan and Keeshana. I have one more question before we get into our actual session today. Cell phones were invented only a few decades ago, and cell phones with cameras were invented even more recently. In the years before that, many people must have seen amazing and beautiful things out and about in the world, but unless they happened to have an actual camera with them, they weren't able to take a picture of it. They weren't able to make a souvenir out of what they saw. Sure, they had it in their memory, so they could visualize it in their mind...but they couldn't share that image with others. And memories fade with time. What did those people do when they didn't have a camera available? What can people do, even today, to capture such a memory? Taylor?"

"Maybe they could paint a picture, or make a drawing of what they saw?"

"Great thinking, Taylor. If they happen to have a sketch book and a pencil, or an easel and canvas and paint with them, they can draw or paint a picture."

Many kids chuckled at that.

"No, I mean it, that was a great answer. They might have brought those things with them with the intention of painting or drawing a beautiful scene during their walk in the woods, or near the seashore, or wherever. Painters and artists do that all the time. You guys are doing a terrific job of really thinking about this. Any other thoughts? Kenny, thanks for raising your hand."

Kenny froze in the headlights. "I forgot," he said.

"That's okay. Raise your hand again if you remember. Gina?"

"You could write down words to describe what you saw. It wouldn't be as good as a photo or a painting, but you could describe what you're seeing with words. And you could even do that after you get home, from memory."

"Another great answer!" he said. "I was hoping someone would say that. All the ideas so far have helped us build a great list of options for capturing beautiful images. I'm here today to talk about poetry. Poetry is totally one more option, one more way of capturing, of describing, how beautiful something looks, or how you are emotionally affected by something or someone. There are many different topics, issues, feelings and sights you can use poetry to describe. Actually, in my opinion, I think writing a descriptive poem is even better than taking a photo, making a drawing, or painting a picture. With poetry, your job is to use words to paint a picture in the mind of the reader, and you have way more than just colors to work with! And you can also describe your feelings, how the beautiful sight made you feel. But we'll talk more about that as we get going here.

"Okay, so today is the first of three poetry sessions I'll be teaching to you 6th graders. Isn't it great how we can open up the walls between classrooms so we can fit you all in here? Anyway, we'll have this poetry session today, and then one each of the next two Fridays. Thank you, Mrs. Vassey, Mr. Lynch-Anderson, and Mrs. Lofthus for allowing me this time with your students to study poetry. Now, I won't be teaching you how to write poetry…your teachers will be doing that. As they've told you, you'll be starting a poetry unit on Monday. My job will be to introduce you to some famous poets, and some famous poetry. Each time I come in, I'll be reading, or reciting, famous poems. Your teachers and I agree that it would be great for you all to hear some poems by Robert Frost, Emily Dickenson, William Shakespeare, and many others. I wish we had more than just three sessions, but those of you who become interested in hearing or reading more…the library has many poetry books for you to check out. And you can find any famous poem or poet online, by googling their name or the name of the poem. If even just one of these poets inspires you, you might choose to seek out more of their poems. And who knows, you might become way more interested in writing poetry yourself."

Mrs. Lofthus raised her hand.

"Yes, Mrs. Lofthus?"

"I just want to say," she said, addressing the students, "we'll be writing a lot of our own poetry over the next two weeks, so even though you won't be doing any writing of poems with Mr. L, he'll be showing you a lot of great tools and strategies you can use to make your poetry more polished. So, welcome, Mr. L…we appreciate you doing these sessions with us. This will be a great addition to the poetry unit we'll be teaching."

"Thank you, Mrs. Lofthus. It's my pleasure to be able to do this with the 6th grade this year. And yes, as I read famous poems to you, I'll point out some of the effective tools and techniques those poets used. And we'll talk about how you can use those tools in the poetry you write.

"So, okay, let's get to today's poet. By the way, after I read each poem, I'll be asking you to tell me your *interpretation* of what the poet is saying, what his or her poem is about. Interpretation is the action of explaining the meaning of something, and one of the cool things about poetry is that poems can mean different things to different people. Anyway, I'll hope to get several of you to *interpret* the poems I'll read. And remember, there isn't a right or wrong answer when you interpret something, so don't be shy about speaking up.

"Oh, and understand that today I needed to do a lot of talking and explaining to introduce you to what we'll be doing during our sessions. The other two days I'm here, we'll be able to start right in on actual poetry. Any questions before I read our first poem?"

Nope.

"Okay, this first poem was written more than two hundred years ago. It was written by a man who, just like we talked about, was out for a nature walk and came to an amazingly beautiful sight he wanted to capture. I think he probably reached for his camera, then probably said something like: 'oh yeah, darn it…cameras aren't invented yet.'"

There was a smattering of chuckles.

"So, this guy had to think of another way to capture the moment. Luckily, he was already a poet, so it was easy for him to use words to describe what he saw. What he wrote down has become one of the most famous poems of all time. His name was William Wordsworth. He was an English poet, a poet from England, who was born 250 year ago. And his poetry is still famous today.

"Okay, so listen carefully as I read his poem. *I Wandered Lonely as a Cloud*, By William Wordsworth. 'I wandered lonely as a cloud, that floats on high o'er vales and hills, when all at once I saw a crowd, a host of golden daffodils; beside the lake, beneath the trees, fluttering and dancing in the breeze. Continuous as the stars that shine, and twinkle on the Milky Way, they stretched in never-ending line, along the margin of a bay. Ten thousand saw I at a glance, tossing their heads in sprightly dance. The waves beside them danced, but they outdid the sparkling waves in glee. A poet could not but be gay, in a such a jocund company. I gazed and gazed, but little thought, what wealth the show to me had brought. For oft, when on my couch I lie, in vacant or in pensive mood, they flash upon that inward eye, which is the bliss of solitude. And then my heart with pleasure fills, and dances with the daffodils.'"

When he finished reading, he paused for a moment to let the poem sink in. "Okay, who would like to start us off, and tell us their interpretation of this poem? Miguel?"

"It's about a man who was out walking through some meadows or fields, and he saw a really huge field of daffodils near a lake, and he thought it was a beautiful sight so he wrote a poem about it to record what he saw, so that other people could see it, too."

"Great interpretation, Miguel. That's a terrific overview of what happened that day, as he described in his poem. Would anyone like to add to that, or offer a different interpretation? Madison?"

"I get the feeling he was feeling kind of bad that day, walking around all lonely, and that the field of daffodils lifted his spirits. I think part of the reason he wrote the poem was not just because it was a beautiful field of flowers, but maybe also because it affected his mood and made him happy?"

"That's an awesome interpretation, Madison. Certainly, the experience lifted his spirits. We know he was lonely…he says so in the first line of the poem. Maybe he was sad too, and the beauty of the daffodils totally changed his emotions that day. Excellent!

"Okay, now let me ask a few specific questions, so we can start to look at some of the tools he used. I know you've all heard of these first two writing tools, but they're important to review…they can really help you paint a vivid picture in the reader's mind. So, in the second stanza, he says this about the large number of daffodils: 'Continuous as the stars that shine, and twinkle on the Milky Way, they stretched in never-ending line.' Who wants to share their interpretation of those lines? Emily?"

"He's saying there's as many daffodils as there are stars in the sky?"

"Excellent! There were *so* many daffodils, he needed to find some over-the-top way to make the reader understand that this wasn't just some big field of flowers. It was immense! He chose to compare them to the number of stars there are in the sky. He's using one of the tools, or techniques, that I want to discuss with you. He's using a *simile* here, comparing how far the flowers stretched to how far the stars stretch across the sky at night. Because he linked them together with the word 'as', it's a comparison called a simile. A simile is a way of describing something by comparing it to something else. A simile does that by using the words 'like' or 'as' when making that comparison. So, for example, if you were writing about a light bulb, and wanted to describe how bright it was, instead of just saying 'the light bulb was bright', you could say 'the light bulb was as bright as the sun'. If you were describing a runner, instead of saying 'he can run fast' you could say 'he can run like the wind'. It just gives your writing more style, more descriptive creativity.

"And as you might know, if the comparison is made *without* using the words 'like' or 'as', it would be a *metaphor*. For example, if you were describing how colorful a girl's painting was, instead of just saying 'her painting was colorful' you could say 'her painting was a rainbow of color'. If you were describing the snow that fell on the playground, instead of saying 'there was a lot of snow on the playground' you might say 'there was a white blanket of snow on the playground'. We'll see more examples of these two techniques next week. They're common tools, but they're very important techniques to keep in your repertoire... in your toolkit.

"Okay, let's move on. In the third stanza, again referring to the daffodils, he says: 'Ten thousand saw I at a glance, tossing their heads in sprightly dance.' He uses another important writing tool here ... another effective technique you can use when *you* write poetry. Do daffodils have heads? Do they really dance? Malcolm?"

"They don't have human heads, but they have *flower* heads," he said. "And they kind of move in the wind and it looks like they're dancing."

"Awesome ... what a great answer. He's using something called *personification* here ... he's giving human qualities to something that's not human, so we can visualize it better, and relate to it better. Notice that he didn't just say 'there were a bunch of pretty flowers blowing around in the wind'. Snoozer! No, he described it as a huge field of daffodils dancing, like people would dance, rocking their heads to the music...like there was a big, colorful party going on. It's a very happy image, and a beautiful image. So, saying the flowers have heads, and saying that they were dancing...both of those are ways he's giving the daffodils human characteristics. Again, that technique is called personification. We'll be seeing more examples of personification in other poems we'll read.

"Okay, we only have about five minutes left today, and there's one more thing I'd like to get to. In the last stanza, he talks about lying on his couch at home, just thinking about stuff; then suddenly he remembered seeing the beautiful daffodils, and that memory made him feel really happy all over again. Cindy?"

"And maybe that's when he decided to write the poem...when he remembered seeing the dancing daffodils? Maybe he wrote it right there on his couch because the memory was so beautiful?"

"What a great thought, Cindy! That certainly might have been when he chose to write the poem. You never know when you'll get inspired to write! Maybe when he recalled how beautiful the scene was, he might have grabbed a pen and said to himself, 'now that's a memory I want to capture and keep forever'.

"Okay, so, in that last stanza, he uses the phrase: 'they flash upon that inward eye'...what does he mean there? Sasha?"

"I think that's the actual moment the daffodils came into his memory, and he could see them again, dancing and swaying."

"Great answer, Sasha! Okay, let's build on that. Who can tell me...why does he call his memory an 'inward eye'? Megan?"

"That's how he's describing how he sees the daffodils in his memory, by looking inward instead of outward?"

"Awesome. Great way to describe that, Megan. When he first saw the daffodils, he was looking outward to see them. Now, he can look inward to see them again...in his memory. Isn't that a cool way he phrases that? And when he sees the daffodils in his mind, his heart fills with joy…just from remembering them and visualizing them. And, check it out, that vision in his mind isn't just a picture…it's a video. In his happy memory, he's dancing with the daffodils.

"Okay, we're almost out of time... you all did an awesome job today! So, to summarize, taking pictures, painting pictures, making drawings, writing poems…all great ways to capture a scene or a feeling. In my opinion, writing poetry is the best choice of all of those. A picture can't make you visualize human qualities on flowers, or look inside someone's mind to let us know that their memories are making them happy, or less lonely. But a poem can do that. Ok, thank you everyone, and thank you, teachers. See you all next Friday!"

During the following week, a few 6th graders stopped by to talk with Mr. L about poetry. They wanted to know who some of his favorite poets were, if he would like to hear some of the poems they'd written, and which poet would be covered in the next session. He was delighted that his session with them had ignited, or perhaps re-ignited, their interest in poetry.

Mr. L was the school's Resource Room teacher, so he taught remedial math, reading, written language, and social skills groups every day. It wasn't often he got the opportunity to teach material from the Arts, so he was happy that his proposal to do so had been accepted by the 6th grade teachers and by the school's principal. It was only for three sessions, but he knew it would be time well spent for everyone involved. He was able to combine his love of poetry with his love of teaching, so this was already making his heart with pleasure fill.

SESSION TWO

"Hello again, everyone," Mr. L said as he looked around the room. "I've been looking forward to this all week. I had the chance to speak with some of you during this week, and I want to say that everyone is always welcome to come talk poetry with me. Or to discuss any other topic, for that matter.

"One of the things I'm getting asked is, whose poems will we be hearing…what famous poets have I chosen? So, today I'll tell you our agenda for today and for next week, so you know who's coming up. Like I said last week, your teachers and I decided that if you hadn't heard of people like William Shakespeare, then it's time that you did. Today's poet will be Robert Frost. We'll hear, and talk about, two of his famous poems. Next week will be Emily Dickenson and William Shakespeare.

"Okay, let's get started. Again, thank you to the 6th grade teachers for allowing me to be here. You have awesome students, and I feel lucky to be able to teach poetry with you all. Okay, Robert Frost. First of all, who's ever heard of Robert Frost, other than me mentioning his name last Friday? Okay, about half of you. So, it's time for all of you to hear about him. Robert Frost was an American poet who was born in 1874, nine years after the Civil War ended. He's best known for his poems about nature and about life in rural areas of the northeast section of the United States. Who can tell me what 'rural' means? Keeshana?"

"It means out in the country, not in a city."

"Exactly right," he replied. "The setting of both of today's poems will be out in the country somewhere. They would be entirely different poems if they took place in a city, so always be aware of the setting when you're reading, or writing, a poem. Even the time of year, and the weather, can be important parts of the setting. Today is the perfect time of year for me to be sharing this first poem. It's a chilly winter day today, so it's just the right time to hear his poem called 'Stopping by Woods on a Snowy Evening'. Actually, I'm going to recite this poem, which means I'm not going to read it, I'm going to tell it to you from memory. I won't be doing that to show off…well, maybe a little. I'll recite it because first, I have it memorized, and second, I think memorizing your favorite poem or poems is good for your brain and your heart. When you read a poem over and over, after a while you'll discover you have it memorized.

"So here we go. And remember, I'll be asking you for your interpretation. Stopping by Woods on a Snowy Evening, by Robert Frost. 'Whose woods these are I think I know, his house is in the village though; he will not see me stopping here, to watch his woods fill up with snow. My little horse must think it queer, to stop without a farmhouse near; between the woods and frozen lake, the darkest evening of the year. He gives his harness bells a shake, to ask if there is some mistake; the only other sound's the sweep, of easy wind and downy flake. The woods are lovely dark and deep, but I have promises to keep; and miles to go before I sleep, and miles to go before I sleep.'"

When he finished, Mr. L paused a moment, then asked for interpretations. Emily?"

"It's about a guy heading home during a snowstorm, riding his horse-drawn sleigh through the woods. He stops for a few minutes to just look at how beautiful the snow is making everything look."

"What a great answer, Emily! That was a terrific summary, interpretation, of what happened in that poem. He stopped to admire the beautiful scene in the woods. After a few minutes he had to leave, but he wanted to capture the moment and never forget it. So, he wrote a world-famous poem about it, so he could re-visit what he was seeing at a later date, and share it with others. Someone tell me about the horse, please. Adeline?"

"The horse was wondering, 'Hey, what's going on, dude? It's snowing…it's like freezing cold out here. Why are we stopping…can we *go* now?'"

"That's such a terrific answer! I'll bet that's exactly what the horse was thinking. He's totally not interested in looking at the beautiful scene, he just wants to get home. Probably thinking 'humans are *so* strange'. Notice that, other than the horse shaking its harness bells, Frost describes the sounds he's hearing. Who remembers what he heard? Nozomi?"

"He heard almost total silence…just a gentle wind and the sound of snowflakes falling, which doesn't make any sound at all. The silence probably added to the beauty of the experience."

"It totally added to the beauty…great answer, Nozomi! Now, that's something a photo or painting can't do…describe the *sounds* of a scene. Remember, Frost wrote about rural places, or out-in-the-country kinds of areas. If they were in the city, there would have been sounds of cars and traffic, and lots of people moving and talking. Vicki?"

"But you said he was born in the 1870's…there were no cars!"

"Excellent point, Vicki. Good thinking! However, he lived a long life, and he wrote the poem in the 1920's, so there were cars by then. Loud, clanky cars. But you couldn't have known when he wrote it, Vicki, so that was great thinking! But back to Nozomi's point…there was almost total silence, which made the experience even more about the simple beauty of nature.

"One more thing, before we move on to another of his amazing poems. One of the creative and fun challenges poets get to have, is finding very cool ways to make their poems rhyme. You all know that poems, at the end of lines, should usually, not always, but usually have some rhyming pattern to them. Roses are red, violets are *blue*, sugar is sweet and so are *you*. Obviously, that's a very simplistic poem, with a simple rhyming pattern. The great poems, or well-written poems, can have much more clever rhyming patterns. *Stopping by Woods on a Snowy Evening* has a very creative pattern that you might not even notice, but it's brilliant. Let's look at the whole poem, which Mrs. Vassey is putting up on the AV screen, thank you, Mrs. Vassey. You'll see that in the first stanza, the first, second and fourth lines all end with words that rhyme: *know, though,* and *snow*. Now, check this out, this is so cool…notice the word at the end of the third line: *here*. That word sets the rhyme for the second stanza, where the first, second and fourth lines all rhyme with '*here*': *queer, near,* and *year*. Then, as you can see, the word '*lake*' at the end of the 3rd line sets the rhyme for the next stanza's first, second and fourth lines: *shake, mistake,* and *flake*. And then the word *sweep* at the end of the 3rd line sets the rhyme in the final stanza for all of the end-of-line words: *deep, keep, sleep,* and *sleep*.

"So how cool is that? It obviously took a lot of creative thinking and planning. I point out the rhyming pattern because, well, first of all, it's brilliant. But also, because when you yourself write poetry, know that creating the rhyming pattern is one more creative challenge for you to hopefully have fun with. It's a useful technique that can make your poetry more refined. Don't be afraid to make your poetry brilliant.

"Okay, any questions before we read and interpret a second Robert Frost poem? Cindy?"

"You said that some poems don't use rhyming words. Does that make them better or worse than poems that rhyme, in your opinion?"

"What a great question, Cindy. It *is* okay for poems to not use rhyming...those poems can be just as effective as rhyming poems. One of my favorite poems of all time is one that doesn't use rhyming. But, as you write poems now, as you're developing your poetry-writing skills, I would suggest that you *mostly* work on having your poems rhyme. Again, hopefully the rhyming aspect makes poetry more fun, different from all other kinds of writing. Miguel?"

"What's the name of that favorite poem of yours that doesn't rhyme?"

"It's called *Ask Me*, by William Stafford. And just a reminder, you can read *Ask Me*, or *any* famous poem, by googling it. You can find and read any famous poem or poet using any search engine.

"Okay, let's move on to his next poem. This one I'll read to you, and then you can give me your interpretations. *The Road Not Taken*, by Robert Frost. 'Two roads diverged in a yellow wood, and sorry I could not travel both, and be one traveler, long I stood, and looked down one as far as I could, to where it bent in the undergrowth. Then took the other, as just as fair, and having perhaps the better claim, because it was grassy and wanted wear, though as for that the passing there, had worn them really about the same. And both that morning equally lay, in leaves no step had trodden black; oh, I kept the first for another day, yet knowing how way leads on to way, I doubted if I should ever come back. I shall be telling this with a sigh, somewhere ages and ages hence; two roads diverged in a wood and I, I took the one less traveled by, and that has made all the difference.'"

After he finished, he said, "Okay, I'm looking forward to your interpretations. Who'd like to start us off? Madison?"

"Okay, he was out walking in the woods, and he came to like a fork in the road, and he stood there for a while and then made his decision to take the one that wasn't used as much as the other one?"

"That's a terrific summary of what happened that day. Great job, Madison! Would anyone like to add to that? Gabriella?"

"I think he chose the one he chose because more people went the other way, and maybe he wanted to go on the road with less people on it so it wouldn't be crowded? Maybe he just felt like being alone that day."

"Awesome thoughts, Gabriella. He certainly went down the road that most people didn't choose. But how did he know? I know at the end, he said: 'I took the one less traveled by', but how could he tell that the one he chose was less travelled on? Ethan?"

"Because that road had more grass growing on it? I guess it was more like a path, or maybe a dirt road?"

"Very good, Ethan. Lots of good points. You're all doing great with this! So, let me ask, why do you think he says that the choice he made, to take that road that fewer people took, has made a big difference in his life? This is a tough one. Trevor?"

"This is kind of thinking outside the box... maybe he met someone important to him when he went down that road, like someone he fell in love with, and so making that choice changed his life in a good way?"

"It's very possible that happened... that's a very good interpretation, Trevor! We can't tell for sure, because he never tells us more about what happened that day, after he chose that road. But that's the cool part about interpreting poetry. In Trevor's interpretation, maybe he meets his future wife, and they live a happy life together. Martine, do you have something to add?"

"I think so. Maybe he was someone that had trouble making decisions...my brother's that same way. Maybe it was hard for him to choose between the two choices, and he was proud of himself for choosing, and maybe that day made him better at making choices for the rest of his life?"

"Another terrific interpretation! And if that was the case, that could very well be what inspired him to write this poem. Thank you for that thought, Martine. Okay, we're getting close to the end of our time here, how about one or two more people. Kenny?"

"I think he...um, I forgot."

"Okay, let me know if you remember. Ok, Daniel...then Megan."

"I think he was proud of the fact that he made a choice that was different than what most other people chose. He wasn't just a follower...he made his own decision."

"Awesome! Very good thinking, Daniel. And, Megan, I can tell by your reaction that you were going to say something similar?"

"Yeah, but I was going to also say that maybe after that day, he became a person who didn't follow others like a sheep, he made his own choices and went his own way in life. Him choosing that unique path that day was kind of like a symbol of how he lived the rest of his life?"

"Wow, that's an amazing thought, Megan...these are all such awesome interpretations! 6th grade teachers, I want to compliment your students once again for their terrific participation, and for sharing such great ideas and interpretations! Great job...isn't poetry cool? Ok, we're out of time, and so I'll see you next week. Oh, and we get fifteen extra minutes next week, so that'll be great. Have a terrific weekend."

During the week, Mr. L sought out Kenny, to have a private conversation with him. He wanted to discuss a few poetry concepts with him regarding the next session. It was apparent to him that Kenny really wanted to participate but lacked the confidence to do so. Mr. L had an idea that might help Kenny feel more self-assured during the next session. He knew that sometimes a little advanced practice (what teachers call 'pre-teaching'), along with repeated rehearsals of how to verbalize a response, can help a student overcome an academic or social challenge.

And he had several visits from kids from all three 6th grade classrooms during the week. He was beginning to see which students might just actually become lifelong lovers of poetry. There are certain kinds of people that just love reading and writing poetry. He was one of them, and he had a feeling there were others blooming out there. For some, he hoped this early exposure to classical poetry might make all the difference.

SESSION THREE

"So, who recognizes the name Christina Rossetti? I see a *lot* of hands, and that's about what I expected. Those of you who were here at Liberty Ridge in 4th grade…you read one of her poems during one of your reading units, and you heard her name at that time. She wasn't on my original agenda, but we have a little extra time today, so I've decided to add her to our session. Christina Rossetti was an English poet, born almost two hundred years ago, in 1830. Remember in our first session, I said that poetry can be about describing beautiful things, but it can also help describe a person's feelings and emotions. She's famous for writing romantic poetry, like about being in love … and also children's poetry.

"The very short poem I'll read for you today is the same one you'd heard in 4th grade, if you were here at the Ridge. If you haven't heard it, well then, today you will. So, *Who Has Seen the Wind*, by Christina Rossetti. 'Who has seen the wind, neither I nor you; but when the leaves hang trembling, the wind is passing through. Who has seen the wind, neither you nor I; but when the trees bow down their heads, the wind is passing by.'"

After he finished, "Okay, first of all, who recognized that poem? Just about all of you. Cool. Who would like to interpret this poem for us? Kenny?"

"I think it's a poem about the wind, and we can't see the wind but we can see what happens when the wind blows things around."

"Excellent answer, Kenny! Great job of getting us started! Who would like to add to that? Sydney?"

"It's a weird poem, 'cause it asks if you've seen the wind. But wind is air, and air is clear and you can't actually see the wind."

"Great addition to the discussion, Sydney. Joaquim, want to add to that?"

"Yeah, like Kenny said, we can't see the wind, but we can see its effects on things, like blowing the leaves on trees, and we can feel it as it goes by. We can prove it's there, but not because we can see it."

"Great answer, Joaquim. Kenny?"

"I agree with what Joaquim said."

"Awesome job of building that interpretation together!" he smiled. "Taylor, want to add to that?"

"If there was a dust storm or something, you could see the wind because it would be all cloudy with dust and dirt. Kind of like if there was an invisible man … we couldn't see him, but if he had mud on him, we could see the mud."

"That's exactly right, Taylor. And great job of using a *comparison* of the wind being like an invisible man! And see, these are the types of conversations and interpretations that poets like to inspire with their poetry. I'm sure Christina Rossetti would be happy with our discussion if she were here.

"Okay, now let's switch over to Emily Dickenson. She was an American poet, born in Massachusetts in 1830, which was the same year Rossetti was born. It was a good year for poets, I guess! She was a very *prolific* poet, meaning she wrote a *lot* of poetry... more than 1,800 poems! She was known for writing poems about good and bad aspects of life and love, and also about mortality. *Mortality* means that we humans recognize that life is short, and that someday, we'll die. It's important to note that she wrote a lot of her poems during the years of the Civil War, a time when a lot of people were dying, which might explain why she was so focused on mortality.

"So, listen carefully, here comes one of her most famous poems. *Hope is a Thing with Feathers*, by Emily Dickenson. 'Hope is a thing with feathers, that perches in the soul; and sings the tune without the words, and never stops at all. And sweetest in the gale is heard, and sore must be the storm; that could abash the little Bird, that keeps so many warm. I've heard it in the chilliest lands, and on the strangest sea; yet never in Extremity, it asked a crumb of me.'

"Okay. This is a tougher one. Who'd like to get us started? Gina?"

"I think it's maybe about hope being a good thing for all of us to have, for all of us to hang onto, because it can help us live happier lives?"

"That's such a great answer, Gina. Hope is such an important thing for all of us ... we should never lose hope, no matter what happens to us. That's for sure a big part of what this poem is about. Nozomi?"

"I wanted to ask, would that be a metaphor she's using, saying that hope is a bird?"

"Yes, excellent observation, Nozomi! This *is* a metaphor she's using.

And isn't it cool, the way she does that…comparing hope to a bird that's perched in our souls? Great job of recognizing that.

"So, let's look more closely at that metaphor: 'Hope is a thing with feathers,' essentially saying that hope is a bird, a bird perched in our soul. And as Gina said, part of what Emily Dickenson is saying is that hope is important, hope can help us…we should never lose hope. Okay, what else does her poem tell us about hope? Keeshana?"

"She says that hope never stops…it'll help us even when it's chilly or stormy outside."

"Excellent insight, Keeshana. And that word 'gale,' in case you don't know, is kind of an old-fashioned way of saying 'strong winds'. So yes, bringing all these ideas together, Emily Dickenson is saying that hope is important, and it's always there for us, even during chilly, stormy, and windy times. Anyone want to add to that?"

No one raised their hand. "Okay, let me ask you this…is hope only helpful and important during bad-weather events? Cindy?"

"Oh, the weather events…the storms and cold…are metaphors for any kind of hardships in life? Like, hope is there for you when you go through tough situations, that there's always hope in any situation?"

"Very good, Cindy! Yes, even the weather events mentioned in this poem are metaphors…they represent, as Cindy said, various hardships we might go through in life. And I'll point out, later in the poem she says that even 'on the strangest sea', hope is there for you…meaning that even when you're feeling lost, not knowing how you'll move forward and find your way, hope is something perched in your soul that will help you get through it all and find your way in life. Awesome discussion, everybody!

"Okay, before we get to William Shakespeare, I want to take a quick inventory of your 'writer's toolbox' and add a few more tools to it. We've already talked about similes, metaphors, and personification being very useful and effective tools for your toolbox. I'm hearing from some of you that you've already been using them during these past two weeks. And that's great…keep on using them! I want to briefly mention two more techniques you should know about, and give a quick example of how they work.

"The first one's called 'onomatopoeia'. It's a long word, going up on the AV screen now, thank you, Mrs. Vassey. Using onomatopoeia can really make your poetry more vivid and expressive. So basically, when you're describing something…you use a word that actually *sounds like* what you're describing. For example, one line from another Emily Dickenson poem is: 'I heard a fly buzz when I died.' If you were reading it out loud, you could really accentuate the sounds in the word: 'I heard a fly buzzzz when I died.' See how the word itself sounds like what you're describing? Isn't that cool? Or, another example might be: 'The tires screeeched when the car took off.' You probably won't use it a lot, but onomatopoeia is a creative and expressive option to have in your toolkit.

"There's one more technique I want to share with you today. 'Peter Piper picked a peck of pickled peppers' is a silly tongue twister, but it uses a useful tool called 'alliteration'. As you can tell, it means having several words with the same starting, or initial, sounds in a line. In that example, it's really overdone, so it would be silly to put a line like that into a poem…unless the whole idea of your poem is to be silly. Here are two examples of alliteration from a famous poem called The Raven, written by Edgar Allan Poe. We unfortunately don't have time to hear the whole poem today, but here are two of Poe's lines that use alliteration: '*Once* upon a midnight dreary, *while* I pondered *weak* and *weary*.' And another line: 'While I *nodded nearly napping*, suddenly there came a tapping.' Using alliteration gives your poems a little extra flair, it demonstrates an extra level of skill as you craft your lines and ideas. But you should use alliteration sparingly. Same with all of these tools, you want to use them every now and then…don't overdo it. Think of them as ingredients in a creative stew…sometimes just a little dash of this or that adds just the right blend of flavors to your poem.

"Okay, and so now we move on to our final poet. Many people say William Shakespeare is the most famous writer of all time, and I would agree with that. He's not really known as a writer of poetry as much as he's seen as a writer of famous plays…like *Hamlet, Macbeth, Romeo & Juliet*, and many others. But in his day, like 500 year ago, he did write many famous poems, called sonnets. Sonnets are one specific type of poem that have 14 lines, that were first used in the 1200's, like 800 years ago! Actually, he published 38 amazing famous plays, and over 150 sonnets, and also some long narrative poems, called epoch poems.

"We've all heard famous quotes from Shakespeare's writings, like: 'To be or not to be, that is the question.' That might be the most famous line ever written…it's a line from Hamlet. Now, check this out, that goes on to say: 'Whether 'tis nobler in the mind to suffer the slings and arrows of outrageous fortune, or to take arms against a sea of troubles and by opposing, end them.' It's like, huh? What the heck does *that* mean? They sure used to talk funny back then. Makes it kind of hard, or even real hard, to understand, and to interpret. It's one of the reasons his works don't get read as much by people these days. Because they're hard to understand. We all know what 'thee' and 'thou art' mean, but most of the language he uses is very foreign to us.

"We're going to look at what is considered to be his most famous sonnet. It's hard to follow, but listen carefully, and I'll guide you through the interpretation. And by the way, look for a metaphor in the very first line, and for some other tools we've discussed. Then we'll take a shot at interpreting, and I'll help you.

"So, *Sonnet 18*, by William Shakespeare. 'Shall I compare thee to a summer's day? Thou are more lovely and more temperate. Rough winds do shake the darling buds of May, and summer's lease hath all too short a date.

Sometimes too hot the eye of heaven shines, and often is his gold complexion dimmed. And every fair from fair sometimes declines, by chance or nature's changing course untrimmed. But thy eternal summer shall not fade, nor lose possession of that fair thou ow'st. Nor shall death brag thou wander'st in his shade, when in eternal lines to time thou grow'st. So long as men can breathe, or eyes can see...so long lives this, and this gives life to thee."

When he finished, "Okay, let's start with the metaphor. Who heard it? Sydney?"

"He's comparing his girlfriend to a beautiful summer day?"

"Great, Sydney. Yes. How many times have you walked outside on a blue sky, sunny day and said 'Wow, what a beautiful day!'? Notice he didn't just say 'Sweetie...you sure are pretty'. He used a comparison, a metaphor...he compared her to a lovely summer day. He even sent up a signal flair to let the reader know that a comparison was coming. And then he goes on to tell her she's even *more* beautiful than a summer day: 'Thou art more lovely and more temperate.' Temperate means calm and mild, it's usually a term used to describe weather or climate. But since he's comparing her to a summer day, he chose to keep going with the weather vocabulary.

"Okay, a couple of lines later, he says: 'Sometimes too hot the eye of heaven shines.' Who wants to take a shot at interpreting that line? Gabriella?"

"Is he talking about the sun? The eye of heaven is the sun, and sometimes the sun makes it too hot outside?"

"Excellent. Again, notice he didn't just say 'sometimes the sun's too darn hot'. He found a unique way of referring to the sun. Great answer, Gabriella. And so, notice that he uses personification twice in that line. When he says, 'the eye of heaven'...he's saying the sun is an eye, *sooo* he's saying heaven has an eye. He's giving heaven, and the sun, human characteristics.

"Okay, how about the line, still talking about the sun: 'and often is his gold complexion dimmed'? Joaquim?"

"Maybe he means that when you look up at the sun, it can kind of blur your vision or hurt your eyes, and makes the sun look dim?"

"That sure happens if you look at the sun ... good thinking, Joaquim. Let's add to that ... okay, Kenny?"

"Yeah, like your eyes might even get tears in them, and make the sun all blurry?"

"Way to add to that idea ... excellent job, Kenny! Patricia?"

"Maybe he's saying that sometimes it's cloudy or hazy out, and that dims the light of the sun? Sometimes, you can even see like the silhouette of the sun through clouds if they're wispy, or if it's hazy."

"Very good, Patricia! We live in Seattle, so we know too well what clouds do to the sunshine. I like your word 'silhouette', where the view of the sun through the haze gets dim. Awesome.

"Now, let's look at the word 'complexion'. Shakespeare says: 'often is his', the sun's, 'gold complexion dimmed'. 'Complexion' is a term used to describe the skin on your face. So, in an indirect way, he's saying that the sun has a face. Personification. He's really being creative, not just saying things the way everyone else would say them. Keeshana?"

"That's like what Robert Frost said and did in his poem, he went his own way and did things his own unique way, right?"

"Absolutely right, Keeshana," he said. "Good remembering, and way to connect the two together. Poetry gives you lots of opportunities to go off-road when you write. It's okay, and preferable, that you create something unique, something that's your own. There's a phrase called 'artistic license', which means writers are given permission to be uniquely creative when they're writing. So, when you're painting an image in the reader's mind, you are totally allowed to color outside the lines.

"We could spend hours discussing just this one sonnet, but we only have time to touch on a few more ideas. He had compared his girlfriend's beauty to a beautiful summer day, so when he then tells her: 'thy eternal summer shall not fade'...what does he mean by that? Cindy?"

"Is he saying that she'll always be beautiful to him, even as she gets older?"

"Excellent! See how he keeps hold of that comparison of her beauty and the beauty of a summer day? And yes, he's saying that she'll always be beautiful, even as time goes by. This is a very romantic poem.

"We have time to discuss one more concept, in the last stanza. The final two lines: 'So long as men can breathe and eyes can see...so long lives this, and this gives life to thee.' This is a tough one...someone want to give it a shot? Nozomi?"

"Even when they get older, as long as he's still alive, and as long as he can still see, she'll still be beautiful to him?"

"Great interpretation, Nozomi. That's a huge part of what he's saying. Let's build on that...would anyone like to add to that, or offer a different interpretation? Megan?"

"I agree with what Nozomi just said, but he seems to be talking about *men* in general, 'so long as men can see'. Is he saying that all men will see her as beautiful even when she's older?"

"Great question. Would anyone like to take a shot at answering Megan's question?" No one raised their hand. "Okay, since we're almost out of time, I'll tell you my interpretation of those last two lines. When he says: 'So long as men can breathe and eyes can see', to me he's saying that, even long after she dies, and after he dies...as long as people are alive on Earth and have eyes to read with...she, and her beauty, will live on forever in the words of this poem. Isn't that beautiful? And in *this* day and age, people who read braille with their fingertips can read about her beauty as well, and anyone who can hear can listen to an audiobook version as well.

"So, Shakespeare has preserved her beauty and her essence, which he shares with everyone who ever reads or hears this sonnet. Remember in our first session...I think it was Megan who said that she'd take a photo of something beautiful so that she could share it with her family and her friends, so they could see the beautiful sight, too? Same thing here…Shakespeare wanted to share maybe the most beautiful thing he'd ever seen. He wanted to share the woman's beauty with others for the rest of eternity.

"Okay folks, we only have three minutes left. I made a short list of some other poets I would recommend…poets you might want to check out. Your teachers will have that list up on the AV screen when you get back from today's assembly. Since we spent our sessions talking about poets from a long time ago, I've included some contemporary poets on the list…poets from more recent years. I hope you'll check some of them out, and that you'll enjoy their poetry as much as I have.

"I want to thank you all for being such amazingly great participants in these poetry sessions! I really enjoyed working with you all. And I have a suggestion. If you find yourself becoming a lover of poetry, you might want to think about finding other people who are also poetry lovers…peers you can share ideas with, share your poetry with. A love of poetry is a cool thing to have in common, and can make for great discussions and friendships. And keep in mind, for you musicians…your poems can be made into songs, too. So, put your artistic licenses to good use…go off-road, paint outside the lines…don't be afraid to astonish yourself with amazing ideas. Have fun reading and writing poetry!"

THE BENEFITS OF
SUCCESS CLUB

"Hello?"

"Hi, Carrie…this is Tammy Reynolds…"

"Hi, Tammy! How nice to hear from you! It's been so long…how are you and Doug and the boys?"

"We're doing pretty well, thanks. And you guys?"

"We're doing well, too," replied Carrie. "We're all pretty happy and healthy."

"I'm glad to hear that," said Tammy. "I miss you and your family!"

"I miss you guys, too. I wish you lived closer so we could get together."

"Actually," said Tammy, "the reason I called…I have some exciting news to share. We're moving back to Bonney Lake next month, so I wanted to let you know that we'll be back in your neck of the woods. In fact, we're moving to the Tehaleh community where you live."

"Wow, that's great, Tammy! You're going to love it here…it's a fantastic community. What section of Tehaleh will you be in?"

"We'll be living near Sprouts Holler Park."

"Then we'll practically be neighbors," said Carrie. "We live in the Pinnacle Ridge neighborhood... less than two miles away."

"That's awesome!" Tammy replied. "I look very much forward to seeing you and Bob and the kids again. It's been what, maybe four years?"

"A little more than that, I think."

"Well, I can't wait to see you. Once we move in, we'll have to get our families together for a dinner or something."

"Absolutely," Carrie replied. "Just let us know when. We'll all look forward to that."

"So will we," said Tammy. "Actually, I have something else I'd like to talk about. Do you have a few minutes to talk about your school there in Tehaleh?"

"Foothills Elementary? Yes, I have time. What do you want to know?"

"I mostly have questions about their special ed program. One of the reasons you and I originally became friends, way back when, was because we both have sons with behavioral challenges. So, since you already know the school that Derek's about to go to, I'd love to pick your brain."

"Sure, pick away! What's on your mind?"

"Okay, let me start with this...though this might be more venting than brain-picking. Derek's been having a very rough year at his school here in Portland. He's constantly been in trouble...refusing to follow directions, not doing any of his work, and being disrespectful to staff. He's been getting recesses taken away, and he gets sent to the principal a lot. He's also disrupting his classroom quite a bit...which is one of the reasons he's sent to the principal so often. It's very frustrating.

"And on top of all that, he also refuses to do any of his homework. And because of that, Tyler and Ben both complain all the time...why do they have to do all their homework while Derek doesn't have to do any? It's a real nightmare. Frankly, Doug and I are hoping that a fresh start at a new school will help change things for him in a positive way. Sorry for venting, but like I said, it's very frustrating. At the very least, it's good to talk with someone who's walked in my shoes. Are you having any of the same kinds of challenges with Tanner?"

"Actually," said Carrie, "I understand, and I *have* walked in your shoes over the years ... so I feel for you. But to tell you the truth, Tanner's doing great at school these days. He's got a pretty terrific work ethic, follows directions, and even gets along fairly well with his classmates. All in all, Bob and I are very pleased with how things are going for him at school."

"Wow, good for you! And good for him! What's your secret?"

"It's no secret, really. The work he's done the last three years with his special ed teacher, Mrs. Daniels, and her team has really set Tanner up for success. And one of the keys to that success, as far as I'm concerned, has been a program they use in their Resource Room called 'Success Club'. I'd be happy to tell you about their special ed program, and about Success Club."

"That would be great!"

"Okay, let me start at the beginning of our own experience. When we moved to Tehaleh three years ago, Tanner was a very challenged boy. All his life to that point, if he didn't feel like doing something, he simply wouldn't do it. He would rarely do any school work or participate in lessons or discussions, and he was often very disruptive in his classroom. But he's learned and grown a *lot* the last three years. So, as you can tell, I'm very pleased with his special ed program."

"Yeah, I can tell; and that's great to hear! Tell me more, please."

"Okay, so let me tell you about Success Club, because to me, that's what's made all the difference for Tanner. And I know the program so well by now, I can describe it pretty fully for you. I know that Mrs. Daniels will tell you all about it once you meet her, but I can give you the highlights now, if you'd like, so you can feel better about what lies ahead for Derek?"

"Yes, please ... again, if you have time?"

"I have plenty of time. Success Club is a motivational program that

Tanner has been involved in every school day for the past three years. It's totally based on inspiring and reinforcing positive behavior…as opposed to punishing bad behavior. It has a two-pronged purpose and benefit, and I have to say that the program has been very beneficial in establishing both structure and motivation for him, at school and at home.

"Anyway, one prong of the program serves to incentivize and motivate students who would otherwise not perform the tasks that they're asked to perform. I'll go into that more fully in a moment, because it's made a hugely positive impact on Tanner's willingness to do work and activities, even when he doesn't want to do them. The second prong is just as important; it serves to lend structure to a student's involvement in his own learning. And since many special education students thrive on structure, as do many general education kids for that matter, this aspect of Success Club has also been very important and effective for Tanner. Let me break down these two main prongs for you.

"I'll start with the 'structure' prong. In essence, every student in Success Club has specific areas of performance to focus on every day…and they know that they'll be consistently rewarded if and when they perform well in these carefully-chosen areas. Mrs. Daniels calls this a 'cognitive structure'…where each kid has a pre-conceived vision of his responsibilities as he begins each day…he knows just what to focus on and achieve in order to earn his rewards. So, kids like Tanner have the advantage of starting each day with very focused goals and motivation.

"I should mention an important point here…every aspect of Success Club gets individually-tailored to fit every kid's unique preferences and challenges, as a way of inspiring them to 'buy-in' to the program. I'll give you several examples, as they apply to Tanner. First, Mrs. Daniels and her team took the time to find reinforcers that Tanner really values…and he was involved in choosing the rewards he can earn. That not only ensured that he would greatly value the rewards, but it perhaps more importantly gave him ownership in the plan from the get-go. Things like candy or treats were not an option; they worked with him to create a list of reward options that were both fun and educationally beneficial. Tanner ultimately chose to earn a few minutes of free time each day that he could use to play educational online games.

"Then Mrs. Daniels met with Tanner's mainstream teacher and me, to determine the four most important behaviors Tanner needs to focus on improving each day. The four most recently targeted behaviors have been 'Following directions', 'Getting started on his assigned task within one minute', 'Staying on task', and 'Completing his work'. You can see how related and interlocked those tasks are, and how important and impactful they would be toward him fulfilling his responsibilities. Those tasks, our goals for him, have changed and evolved several times over the years … his first set of tasks when we arrived three years ago were focused on him becoming verbally appropriate, and non-disruptive, in his classroom and in school … but I'll talk more about that in a bit.

"So, back to how Success Club works. Tanner has a scoring sheet … a daily record, that his mainstream classroom teacher keeps at her desk. All scores he receives reflect his performance in his mainstream classroom. To make things simple, and black and white, Tanner earns a score of either '0', '1', or '2' for each of the four targeted behaviors at the end of every half-day. A '2' means he did a great job of fulfilling his responsibilities, a '1' means he did a pretty good job, and a '0' means that his performance did not meet their expectations in that particular category during that half-day timeframe.

"He has 'Success Club' on his schedule every day from 11:40 to 11:50 … the ten minutes just before lunch, and then again at the end of the day from 3:50 through 4:00. So, at 11:38, and then again at 3:48, he goes up to his teacher to get his scores for each half-day segment. He then takes that scoring sheet to the Resource Room, where Mrs. Daniels goes over his scores with him, discusses any '1s' or '0s' with him, and congratulates him for the '2s' he earned.

"The scores he brings at the end of every half-day translate into the amount of reward time he immediately receives. Every '2' becomes two minutes of free time he can spend playing educational online games; every '1' earns one minute, and of course any '0' earns no minutes. So, for example, half-day scores of '2, 1, 0, 2' would earn him five minutes of reward time. When he gets all '2s', he hands the sheet to Mrs. Daniels and she just says something like 'totally awesome, way to go...get right to your reward time!', and he'd get to spend the entire eight minutes online playing his game. For any '1s' or '0s', she and he would first spend the non-reward minutes discussing why he got the lower scores, and how he could make better choices going forward. After the discussion, he would receive the remaining minutes of reward time. If he ever gets two or more '0s', he would not receive any reward minutes for that particular session...she and he would instead spend the entire time discussing what happened, and how the next half-day could be more successful. The same would be true if he scored just one '0', but on two or more consecutive half-days.

"Oh, and this is important...before he gets his reward game minutes, he gets to put up stickers on his own personalized thermometer graph. For every point he scores, he gets to put one sticker onto his rising graph. The stickers on the graph represent his progress toward a long-term reward he'll earn when he eventually reaches the top of the thermometer. And when he reaches the top of one graph, another blank one is put up beside it, and he starts right into filling the next one.

"Let me go back to what I just said about Tanner having 'personalized' thermometer graphs. All facets of this club get personalized, actually...looking to make students as excited and invested as possible. It's sort of like a marketing campaign; there's a lot of glitz and perks and fanfare...and salesmanship on the part of the staff."

"I'm not sure I understand," said Tammy. "What do you mean by 'personalized'...can you give me some examples?"

"Sure. It's lots of little, subtle things that add up...they make the kids feel like the program was made just for them. I already mentioned Tanner had a hand in choosing his rewards. He also got to choose the color of his daily scoring sheets, the one used by his classroom teacher...and he also helped design the header of that sheet. His favorite color is pink, so his sheets are pink. He also chose the color of his thermometer graphs, also pink, and then he got to choose the stickers that he gets to place on his rising graph. Tanner loves frogs, so Mrs. Daniels got him a large supply of various 'tree frog' stickers that he gets to put on his graph every day. All of these little personalized nuances make a *big* difference; they give him tons of buy-in and ownership in his membership to the club. Part of this, too, is that Tanner feels like it's a privilege to be a member, and that he needs to do his part to keep up his membership. It just...works for him, and I'm delighted it does."

"I can see why you would be," said Tammy. "Thank you for explaining that...please continue."

"Anyway, Tanner's graphs are taped up inside the coat closet doors in the Resource Room, so they are his own private graphs. Mrs. Daniels keeps every one of his graphs up all year long, so he can see all the progress he's made...he can see his huge, growing collection of tree frogs. When he fills up the coat closet doors, she moves some of his graphs to the inside of other cabinet doors to make room for the new ones. He got a big kick out of it when Mrs. Daniels lightheartedly 'complained' to him for making his graphs 'overflow out of the coat closet', and that his graphs were 'taking over the room'. He speaks about his graphs with pride at home, and loves to show them off to me or to Bob when we're at the school. We love it when he feels so proud of himself...and of course we're very proud of him, too!

"I have to tell you about this other kid's graphs...that are inside different cabinet doors in the Resource Room. Nathan is also a student with behavioral challenges, and because he's been in behavioral skills groups with Tanner for a few years now, they've become pretty good friends. Anyway, Nathan loves trains... new ones and also old, kind of antique, trains. Mrs. Daniels did online searches and found a hobby store somewhere in the Midwest that sells booklets of stickers of new and old train cars. So, on Nathan's graphs, these train cars are all 'hooked' to one another, up one graph and then over to the next graph, like one long train…it's very cool to see! I've been in the Resource Room a few times during end-of-day Success Club, and Nathan, like Tanner, loves to show me his graphs. Those boys love to see the colorful representation of their successes…all on display inside the cabinet doors."

"That sounds so cool," Tammy said. "Are Tanner and Nathan friends outside of school? I tell you, I'd give my right arm for Derek to start having friends to do things with…that would be so beneficial on so many levels."

"Well, he'll certainly have Tanner as a friend up here, right from the start. I think they'll remember each other? We should plan some carefully chosen activities we can get them to do together…maybe as our families have get-togethers, to get them off on the right foot.

"But, to answer your question about activities outside of school…yes, his mother Shannon and I have taken the boys out for pizza together quite a few times. She and I both augment Success Club rewards with our own 'at home' rewards…to further bolster the effects of the reinforcement. Nathan is also a kid who totally buys in to the program, as much as Tanner does. Mrs. Daniels encourages all parents to find ways to augment the rewards of the program; to give long-term rewards for great performance by their kids. So, Shannon approached me with the idea of doing a 'joint' long-term reward together, and I jumped at the idea. When both boys have filled five graphs, they get to have a 'pizza prize' together. One of the boys always ends up needing to wait a bit for the other to finish their fifth graph, but we see 'learning to be patient' as an important skill for them to develop as well. Her idea has worked out great on many levels, including the friendship the boys have. And, and this was unintentional but it's worked out very well…the small amount of competitiveness they each feel as they race to be the first one to finish their graphs adds a little extra spark of motivation for them as they do their work every day."

"That was such a great idea on Shannon's part," said Tammy. "I imagine parents' involvement can make a big difference in how effective Success Club can be. I'm sure both of you ladies are a big part of why your boys are so invested. Good for you both! Okay…I got us off on a tangent there…so, please…continue."

"Okay. So, as I'd said earlier, Tanner also gets to work toward his own long-term goal as he builds-up each graph. When he gets to the top of every graph, he gets an extra five-minute bonus of reward time. This reward time is given during his behavioral skills group time when he's in the Resource Room in the early afternoon. It usually takes about a week and a half or so to fill each graph, and Tanner can always tell you at any given moment how many frogs he's got up, and how many more he'll need to reach the top.

"One more thing…for every session of Success Club, if Tanner chooses to forego his immediate reward, he can instead add two more stickers onto his thermometer graph for every five minutes of reward time he gives back. This allows him to learn to 'save' for the future…to give up short-term gains for long-term benefits. Something some adults are not great at doing. Having long-term goals and rewards to consider makes Tanner really think about his options and strategies each day. I have to say, he's taken advantage of this 'save for the future' nuance quite a few times…and I see this as a mindset that'll serve him well later in life.

"So, you can see that Success Club has a lot of beneficial aspects to it, and the students are made to feel like it's quite a privilege to be a member. Every facet is delivered with enthusiasm and fanfare, and Tanner is totally and happily immersed in his membership. Oh, by the way...at the end of each school year, he gets to bring home all of his graphs for the year, and we've made a spot to display them on a bulletin board in our garage. So, he gets to bask in the glory of his accomplishments over summer breaks that way. He's really quite proud of his successes in Success Club...and so are we."

"See...I was right," said Tammy. "You parents that go the extra mile obviously have a huge impact on how invested your kids become! It sounds like you do such a great job with him, Carrie! I think I'm going to learn a lot from you."

"Nice of you to say...thank you, Tammy. As you know, the job of being a parent of a child with behavioral challenges isn't easy, so we're always looking for any advantages we can find. As you're doing right now for Derek, I might add. I think you and I are going to learn a lot from each other in the years ahead."

"I think you're right," Tammy said. "I'm sure you're right."

"One last thing," said Carrie. "They don't just have students with behavioral challenges in Success Club; there are several other special education students involved as well. The structure, the individualized-tailoring, and the consistency of doling out rewards works well for all of them, I'm told. I happen to think that any parents with a kid who needs to improve their behaviors, motivation and work skills can make use of the techniques and benefits of this program, whether their kid is in special ed or not. I hear that there are one or two families from our school that have implemented their own 'at home' version of the structure and reward system of Success Club.

"So, anyway, there you have it...my overview of Success Club. I'm sure I left out some important things, but I think I covered all the larger aspects...the highlights. I know Mrs. Daniels will give you all the details when you meet with her."

"Thank you so much for all of that information!" Tammy said. "That gives me a lot of hope for what lies ahead. I have other questions about the school in general...the staff, the principal, the schedules...but let's save that for another conversation. I've taken up enough of your time today. But really...this has been so helpful, Carrie...thank you!"

"You're more than welcome, Tammy," said Carrie. "I will say...the principal and the entire staff at Foothills are awesome...they're very progressive and professional. I know you'll be very happy...but as you say, we can discuss all that at length in our next conversation."

"There'll be so many great things happening in the next weeks and months," said Tammy. "Moving back to Washington, moving into our new house, seeing you and your family...and, of course, getting started at Foothills. So much to look forward to."

SCHOOL SAFETY
CONCERNS

"You've *got* to be kidding me," I said. "You're actually considering making this a policy? So, let me make sure I understand what you're saying here…you would have us keep our doors closed and locked…even if a kid might still be out in the hallway?"

"That's exactly what I'm saying," said Carolyn. "During an intruder lockdown, once you've checked the hallway and gathered in all the students in the immediate area outside your door, your door gets locked…and it needs to *stay* locked for the safety of all the students in your room. If there's a dangerous intruder in the building, re-opening your door to let in one child could let the intruder into your room, risking the lives of all the students, and adults, in the room."

"So," I replied, "let's just say there's a little girl who was in the bathroom when the lockdown was announced over the intercom. If she doesn't get back in time, before we lock our doors…she gets left out in the hallway? She gets back, bangs on our door, and we have to say, 'Sorry, we can't let you in, good luck out there'…really?"

"I know that sounds terrible," she conceded, "but what if the intruder has a gun? Letting him into your room, full of students, could be devastating. We have to make sure that never happens. And, we have to consider the possibility that the intruder is either following this girl, to see which door will open for her, or that he's threatened her, telling her to knock on a door…maybe a specific door that he's targeting. I know it's an unspeakable decision to ask teachers to make, but we feel it's the safest thing to do."

"I'm not sure anyone on our staff would actually follow that policy," I said. "Hell, I don't think *I* would."

"I understand,' she said. "It goes against every instinct a responsible, caring adult has. But that's got to be our policy. That's *going* to be our district's policy."

"Okay, let's say for a moment that we fully embrace that policy. What's to keep the intruder, who wants to get into classrooms, from, say, pulling the fire alarm? Will part of the new policy be…if the fire alarm goes off during an intruder lockdown, everyone should ignore the fire alarm?"

"That's a very good point," she replied. "Yes, I suppose we'll need to make that part of the policy, too."

"Okay, so what happens if there really is a fire during a lockdown, maybe set by the intruder?"

"Well, now you're getting into potentialities that are beyond the scope of this discussion," she said. "I mean, what happens if there's an *earthquake* in the middle of a lockdown? We can't account for every combination of occurrences for every situation."

"I guess you're right. But actually, isn't that part of our job…to think of as many potential occurrences, and worst-case scenarios as possible?"

"I know you're new to this, Dean," she said, "and I appreciate your passion about safety. But understand that you'll need to do these things one step at a time. You'll need to get a solid system of policies in place, accounting for obvious circumstances, and work from there."

"I understand...one step at a time."

"Right," she said. "I'll need to get going soon...I have other calls I have to make. So, tell me what's on your agenda for tomorrow's Safety Team meeting?"

"Our main goal will be finishing up the details of our new catastrophic-emergency plan, the one Jillian and I will be explaining to parents in the video we're going to post on our school's website."

"Oh yeah, how's that coming along?"

"Really well, actually. She and I are meeting after school today to work on the script...we're pretty close to being done."

"You guys rock over there at Glacier Ridge! Making and posting a video is an excellent idea...I really look forward to seeing it when it's done. I might recommend that all schools do that. Hey, I have to get going. Good luck with everything...have a good evening."

"Thanks...you too."

After school, I gathered up my Safety Team binders and went over to the conference room. When I walked in, I was surprised to find Jillian already hard at work...her papers and files spread out on the table.

"You don't mess around," I said.

"Oh, I just got here...I only got about a five-minute head start on you. It just *looks* like I've been here for hours. I'm thinking we can get most of this done today. I'm looking forward to recording the video soon."

"Me too. It's great when things are important and fun at the same time. How often do we get to do that? Okay, so let's get to it..."

We worked until around 5:15. I leaned back and stretched, "Okay, I'm starting to run out of work ethic here...how are you doing?

"I think this would be a great time to stop," she replied. "I'm thinking one more session like this and we'll be ready to start our film career."

"Sounds good to me…I'm looking forward to it. Hey, since we've been creating dialogue here about dealing with intruders, I want to share a quick story with you about something that happened to me this past summer. You got a few minutes to hear this?"

"Absolutely."

"Okay, so this was back on August 9th…I think I'll always remember the date. It was just after 2:30 in the morning; I woke up when I heard a sound outside my bedroom window, like a scratching sound. I listened for a few seconds, trying to figure out what it was… then the motion detector lights came on outside, and the noise stopped. I laid awake for a few more minutes, just listening, but everything was quiet. But then the lights turned back off, and the scratching sound started right back up again. Kind of sounded like maybe a cat was scratching at my window screen? My curtains were drawn closed, and of course the room was dark, so I couldn't see what was going on. But the sound was right outside my window.

"So, I got out of bed and started walking toward the window. I was thinking I'd go open the curtains and yell at the cat or squirrel or whatever, and scare it away. But something in my foggy brain made me rethink that plan…I went to my closet first and grabbed a baseball bat, just in case. Then I started walking back toward the window. I was only like maybe three feet away from getting to the curtains, when I heard the window slide open behind the curtain! I froze in place…but I was suddenly wide awake! The curtains were still closed, so at that moment I couldn't see who'd opened the window. But a few seconds later, I saw a head and shoulders start to take shape in the fabric of the curtains as the guy started coming in head-first through the window. From the time I'd heard the window slide open, to the time I started to see his form taking shape in the curtain, only about maybe five seconds had gone by. But during that time, I had frozen solid, I couldn't move…now I know what the word petrified really means. But fortunately, him starting to crawl in through the window made me unfreeze, and without even thinking I hit him right on the head with the bat. He fell back out of the window, and I yelled 'quick, call the police!' even though I was the only one in the house."

Jillian leaned forward, "Wow, that is so scary! So, then what happened?"

"I grabbed my phone off the nightstand and called 911 and stood near that window with my bat until the police got there...it was only like a few minutes. After I told them what happened, they checked all around my house and yard. They asked me to come outside, and they showed me the rectangular section of screen the guy had cut away to gain access to my window...that was the scratching sound I'd heard.

"They never caught the guy, but he ended up with a big lump or gash on his head for his troubles. For the next week or so, whenever I was out and about, like at the grocery store or wherever, I checked out everyone's head and forehead for lumps or bandages."

"Ever wonder what you would have done if you saw a guy with a big lump on his forehead?" Jillian asked. "Think you would have asked him how he got hurt, or if he'd broken into any houses lately?"

"I'm not sure what I would have done. You know though, when I think back on it, he and I were both *real* lucky that night. I hadn't been expecting the sound to turn out to be a person, so I was carrying the bat hanging down near my feet...and I ended up hitting him like I was swinging a tennis racket with one arm. I think if I had been holding the bat up on my shoulder, and hit him with both arms, with all the adrenaline of the moment, I might have split the guy's head open or killed him or something. That would have been terrible.

"And also, if I hadn't woken up when the scratching sound started, or if he had chosen a different window in any other room in the house...or if I had laid in bed one more minute before deciding to get up, he would have gotten into my house, and who knows what would have happened then. So, I was lucky in a lot of ways. And you know, I think that experience inspired me to agree to co-chair the Safety Team this year. It's funny how traumatic experiences can influence your choices in life…

THE VIDEO

"Hello, everyone. My name is Dean Lawrence. I'm here today with Jillian Maglena to share information with you regarding our new and improved safety plans and procedures here at Glacier Ridge Elementary. Miss Maglena, as many of you know, is our ELL teacher. She works with English Language Learners at our school…students who are learning to read, write, and speak English as a second language. And, as you might know, I'm the special education Resource Room teacher at the school. But we both wear another hat here at our school…we're the co-chairs of the Glacier Ridge Safety Team."

"Hi everyone," Jillian said. "The Safety Team has been working hard all year to establish and implement new safety policies and procedures. This video will describe the steps we've taken to make sure we're prepared for any type of emergency situations at our school. Our Safety Team, and our entire staff, take school safety extremely seriously. There is no more important job for us at our school than keeping your children safe."

"All members of our Safety Team," I said, "have taken online training through FEMA's Emergency Management Institute to stay at the forefront of the latest and most effective emergency response techniques. Our team meets every month, to continue to develop and improve our school's safety plans. As you'll discover in this video, there are many and various types of emergencies and safety concerns for us to be prepared for."

"We feel it's important to keep you informed to the fullest degree possible when it comes to the safety measures we're putting in place here at Glacier Ridge," Jillian added. "We'll go through the various drills and procedures with you step by step, and describe each one fully. Many of you parents are often in our building on school days; you might be here during some of our many scheduled drills, and this will serve to let you know what to expect.

"We're even going to walk you through a mock catastrophic-emergency drill on this video," she added. "We'll describe all of the procedures involved, from evacuating the building, to keeping your children safe throughout the duration of the emergency, to reuniting you with your children when the emergency is over. We want you to know everything we're doing to keep your children safe."

"The particular catastrophic-emergency process we're going to walk you through," I said, "will simulate the after-effects of a major earthquake, like a 7.5 or so … one that would bring down structures and cause extensive damage. We'll describe the steps we would take: the 'drop-cover-hold on' steps used during the shaking, followed by the safe evacuation of everyone from the building, the setting up of various stations around the school grounds, the setting up of a Medical Station to deal with injuries, and even the staging of our Search and Rescue Team, whose job it would be to go back into the building to, well, search for anyone trapped inside and rescue them.

"I have to admit, when we first contemplated ideas like having a Search and Rescue Team, and a full-blown Medical Station, I thought, 'We don't need to do all that; we're an elementary school full of hundreds of kids. Surely, emergency responders from the city and state would swarm to our aid in the event of a major natural disaster.' But when you think about it, we might be one of hundreds of schools impacted across the area, not to mention hospitals and senior care facilities, retirement homes, government facilities, day care centers, buildings in cities that might collapse, and so on. In such a widespread major catastrophic event, it could be many hours, or maybe even days, before outside emergency responders could get to our school to help us. That's why we need to be prepared, to the fullest extent possible, to deal with such an event. We have to be ready for worst-case scenarios! That's why our Safety Team spends so much time preparing these procedures; and why members of our team get FEMA certified."

"But before we talk about that catastrophic-emergency process," Jillian said, "we'll give you an overview of each of the more typical emergency situations we've prepared for, and walk you through the basic steps involved.

"We'll start with the basic fire drill. These drills are something we adults have all been through ourselves back in our own school days. These have always been the most common school drills, practiced often during the school year. Every classroom always evacuates to the same designated spot on the playfield. Each line forms at the back end of the playfield, as far away as possible from the building. All classroom teachers have 'safety backpacks' that they grab and bring with them as they evacuate; those packs hold all of their classroom data, and their up-to-date rosters. They make a careful count of their students, and have signal flags to indicate that everyone is accounted for, or if there's anyone missing.

"In the event of an actual fire, we would be in close contact with our local fire department, who would of course take charge when they got to our school. They would let us know when and if it would be safe to return to the building. We'll be talking more, later in this video, about steps that would be taken if students aren't allowed back in the building…if they need to be kept safe and secure for an extended period of time before going through the processes involved in reuniting them with their parents to go home."

"The next drill we'll discuss will be an earthquake drill," I said. "Now, as we'd mentioned earlier, we'll be walking through an entire mock earthquake drill that will simulate our follow-through if the earthquake was a devastating, major quake that levelled buildings around the area. But for the moment, we'll discuss a more routine earthquake drill...response to a minor quake that would allow us to return to the building in short order. So, when an earthquake drill happens, we don't use the alarm...that's only used for fire drills. Instead, the office, Principal Montlake if she's in the office, or other office staff if she's not, would use the intercom to notify everyone. They'd say, 'This is an earthquake drill. Everyone please drop, cover, and hold on'. We have practiced that procedure a lot, and I'm sure you've all perhaps practiced those steps at home? We would encourage you all to practice that at home. Students are asked to *Drop*: crawl under their desk; *Cover*: cover their head and neck with one arm, then *Hold On*: use their other arm's hand to hold on to a leg of the desk, to stabilize the desk. They get under desks, of course, in case anything from the ceiling falls down...that protects them from being hit. After a few minutes...after the shaking stops in a real event, the office would notify everyone to evacuate the building. Teachers bring their safety backpacks, and the same procedures are used as we described for fire drills, to make sure all students have evacuated to the play field, and are accounted for. When the danger is determined to be over, with no structural damage to the building, everyone would be allowed back inside.

"And by the way, every teacher has an assigned 'buddy teacher' for this type of situation; someone right next door to their classroom. These teachers would check in with one another to make sure no one has been incapacitated during the quake. If a teacher has, say, been knocked unconscious because something fell on them, the buddy teacher would evacuate students from both of their classrooms, and then immediately send help back for the injured teacher."

"The next drills we'd like to discuss are lockdown drills," said Jillian.

"There are actually two different kinds of lockdown drills, and we think it's important to make sure everyone knows the distinctions between them. You might hear on the news that a school or a district has gone into 'lockdown'…so we want you to know specifically what that means, depending on which type of lockdown is being implemented. The difference lies in how imminent the danger is. In one situation, there is a perceived dangerous person in the general area of the community. In the other situation, that dangerous person is already inside your building.

"The first of those situations is referred to as a 'general lockdown'. Say, for example, a bank was robbed in our region of the city, and the armed thieves are on the loose in the general area. Until those robbers are apprehended, or until the police give the okay, the schools in the district would all lock their exterior doors, so no one can get into the building. Activities inside the school would proceed as normal. Classroom doors would not be locked, schedules and activities would not change. Every exterior door at the school would be locked, and those doors would be monitored by staff. No one would be allowed to enter or exit, but everything else would continue as normal inside the school. When local officials notify the district that the outside threat has been eliminated or contained, then the exterior doors would be unlocked and people would again be allowed to enter and exit the building."

"The other type of lockdown is far more alarming and dangerous," I said. "This would be an 'intruder lockdown'. This means that a dangerous person is already in the building. So, when the office states over the intercom: 'We are in an intruder lockdown, I repeat, an *intruder* lockdown,' every teacher would spring into immediate action. We'd all do a very quick check outside our classroom door, and tell any students in the hallway near our room to come immediately into our room. It doesn't matter if they're from a different classroom, we'd bring them immediately into our room. Once students in the immediate area of the hallway are inside, the classroom door gets closed and locked. Once locked, those doors do not get unlocked for *any* reason, until the danger is eliminated and an eventual 'all clear' is given by police or by office personnel.

"The curtains on the door get closed, so that the intruder can't see inside the room. Students and adults are moved to the safest part of the room, away from windows and doors. All blinds on windows get closed tight, in case the intruder has gotten outside of the building. Everyone would stay inside for as long as necessary, until the all-clear is given by local authorities.

"And so that you know, all classrooms and specialty rooms have a stored supply of food and water, and rudimentary toiletry equipment and items, in case classrooms need to stay locked-down for extended periods of time."

"The next drill we'd like to discuss is a 'shelter-in place' drill," Jillian said. "This procedure is used in the event that chemical, biological, or radiological contaminants get released in the building. The office would use the intercom to say, 'This is a shelter-in-place emergency…everyone please follow shelter-in-place procedures immediately.' Teachers would do a hallway sweep and tell any students in the hallway near our room to come immediately into our room. As with the intruder drill, it doesn't matter if students in the hallway are from a different classroom, they'd be brought into the nearest classroom. Our custodian would turn off all fans, all ventilation…including heating or air conditioning. All students and adults would remain inside locked classrooms…or whatever room they had been in, such as the Library, Resource Room, etc. Teachers would seal all windows, doors, and vents with duct tape and plastic sheeting that's already been cut to size. Everyone would stay where they are until authorities are able to determine that the air is safe to breathe. Since a clean-up process might be necessary, everyone might be asked to stay sheltered-in-place for an extended amount of time."

"So, those are the types of emergency situations we wanted to talk with you about," I said. "We thought it was important to share the various types of situations, and what they're called. We recognize that terms like 'shelter-in-place' and 'lockdown' are often confused with one another, as are the two different kinds of lockdowns, of course. We wanted to be specific in identifying each so that you know what they are."

"Okay," said Jillian, "now we want to turn our attention to describing our procedures for the catastrophic-emergency situation we mentioned. Like we said, we're going to walk you through what would happen if there was a major earthquake, one that would damage our school and other buildings in the area, and leave us stranded out on the school grounds for several hours or more.

"We'll put this map of the school grounds up now for you, so you can see the layout of where all of our team stations will be set up. It was apparent to us that we needed to create a logical, workable flow, from teams picking up needed materials and supplies from our safety materials pod, to setting up tables and equipment for our various stations, to setting up bathrooms with privacy tarps, to allowing for close, continual supervision of all students, to setting up medical facilities. And doing all of that while also preparing for the transfer of students to parents who arrive to pick them up. We'll briefly address each station now, and discuss what they're for and where they'll be located."

"Now," I said, "we anticipate that in a real emergency of this kind and magnitude, most of you parents would of course be arriving to check on, and pick up, your children. Part of the reason we're going over this process with you now is so you'll know what we'll be doing… because there's a very good chance that you'll be asked to stand in line on the other side of our chain link fence, watching and waiting as events unfold. We want you to know that even during that nerve-wracking time, we'll be taking great care of your children.

"So, we want to thank you ahead of time for the patience you'll be asked to demonstrate as we go through the various processes we're about to describe. Understand that we can't just start passing children along to adults that show up...there's a rigorous and extensive system of checks and double-checks to make totally sure every child gets released to the proper adults...and this vetting system takes time. So again, thank you in advance for being patient while we're making sure every child is kept safe...not just from the natural disaster, but also from the possibility of leaving with the wrong adult.

"Okay, let's start with the Medical Station. This station will be assembled right outside the portable buildings at the north edge of the playground. It'll be staffed by the school nurse and two other staff members who have first aid certification. If the need arises, there are other first aid certified staff members from other teams that can be rotated to this station. While we won't have a doctor available, our team will be able to administer first aid to any students and adults with minor injuries. For major injuries, we would call for an ambulance, and take care of those injuries to the best of our abilities until the ambulance arrives."

"Now, let's talk for a moment about the Materials and Construction Team," said Jillian. "They'll be responsible for efficiently distributing the materials and supplies from the large safety materials pod as teams arrive, and then they'll help in the assembly of team stations, like the Medical Station and the Parent/Student Reunion Station. They will also assemble the bathroom areas and privacy curtain tarps. By the way, we'll be using the big toy area for the bathroom area, so we can set up rudimentary toilets and hang tarps on existing structures to create bathroom stalls."

"Okay, let's discuss the Search and Rescue Team," I said. "They'll be responsible for first gathering their equipment from the safety pod...things like first aid kits, pry-bars, hard hats, gloves, and their assignment logs, which show their designated rooms to search. As they search the building, they'll have signs to tape to each room's door, indicated that the room has

been checked and cleared, or that there's someone needing medical attention. Team members have had first aid training, so they can assist anyone
with minor injuries they might find in the building."

"The Student Supervision Team is the team the majority of the
teachers and paraeducators get assigned to," said Jillian. "It'll be like
they've walked all their students out onto the playfield for a fire drill, but
then they'll need to watch over their students...keeping them cued up
in their lines...for perhaps a long time, several hours maybe. Kids can sit
on the grass while they're in line, but it's important that they stay in their
lines so that we can always account for where *every* child is at every moment. If kids need to go to use a restroom, they'll need to sign those kids
out...noting where they went and when they left, and then sign them
back in when they return. There will also be a central dispatch station...a
central table set up in front of the lines, with two teachers assigned to
also keep track of every child...they'll be the ones who'll process paperwork and allow students to go use the bathrooms, or to leave the field to
be escorted over to be released to their parents."

"Which brings us to the next station," I said, "which is the Parent/
Student Reunion Station. This is the team you'll interact with when you
come to pick up your children. We want you to know exactly how the
process will work when you get here. That station will be set up just inside the gated rear entrance to the school grounds; just off the rear parking lot. There will be clear signage that will guide all parents up toward
the processing tables, where three different lines will form according to
the *student's* last name: "A through G', 'H through O', and "P through Z'.
Please understand that there will probably be long lines, and, again, that
we'll be carefully vetting every single request for the release of children
to parents. Not every parent is legally allowed to pick-up their children
from school. Friends and neighbors of children will *not* be allowed to
leave with children who are not their own kids. This will take time...so
again, thank you ahead of time for your patience."

"So, the process will look like this," Jillian said. "When you arrive at the table after standing in line, you'll go through the vetting process to verify that you are a parent that is permitted to leave with the child or children you're requesting. Once you get approved, the staff member working with you will make out a 'transfer request' card for your child or children. That card will get taken across the blacktop by a staff member, to the Student Supervision Team's central table at the front edge of the field. The card will be like a requisition card…requesting that the listed student or students be released…to be escorted over to the Reunion Station to be re-united with their parents."

"And that brings us to the Command Team," I said. "This team will be centrally-located between all of the stations, overseeing the flow of all operations. The Command Team will consist of our principal, Dr. Montlake, and several staff members, including Miss Maglena and myself. All members of this team will have multiple duties, including serving as liaisons to specific stations. For example, if the Medical Team needs further assistance, their liaison will arrange for other staff members to rotate to the Medical Station. If ambulances are needed, the liaison will liaise with the Command Team to arrange for that."

Jillian jumped in, "If Search and Rescue needs assistance in the building, the liaison for that team will arrange for staff to rotate to give that assistance. Their liaison would also be in charge of deploying the Search and Rescue Team members to other duties if search and rescue is either not needed, or is unable to occur because the building is not safe to enter.

"Meanwhile, Dr. Montlake will make executive decisions regarding all of the above. She, and our office manager, Mrs. Smithers, will be the ones making contact with outside agencies, requesting ambulances and emergency responders, if any are available to respond. They will also make sure all facets of all teams are working in a coordinated and systematic fashion, with the assistance from other Command Team members, of course.

"As you can see, our various teams have a lot of moving parts, and making sure everyone is working in concert with one another takes a lot of work and coordination. Our Command Team members, and all of our teams, are prepared and ready to take on that challenge."

"So, that's our overview of our school's safety procedures," I said. "Take comfort in knowing that we will continue to do whatever it takes to keep your children safe. It's our most important job, and our number one priority. You trust us to keep them safe, and we take that responsibility very seriously.

"Thank you for listening, everyone; we hope this information has been helpful. Always feel free to contact us at the school with any questions or comments. So, on behalf of Miss Maglena, Dr. Montlake, our Safety Team, and our entire staff, all the best to you and your families. Stay safe and healthy, everybody!"

ISABELLA'S SIGHT VOCABULARY

"Yes, it's a strategy you can use when you're reading to Isabella," I said. "It's a great way to make extra-effective use of that reading time over the summer, and it will really help her become a much stronger reader. I'll be happy to send you an email that'll describe the technique, and explain the reasoning behind the strategy…"

Hi Sadie,

It was nice talking with you on the phone this morning. Here's a summary of what I'd suggest you work on with Isabella over the summer, along with some reading strategies I'd recommend that you use. I'll be happy to be your on-going teammate this summer…if you keep me posted as to how things are going, I'll make further recommendations as she progresses. I'm sending this from my home email, so we'll be able to communicate over the summer, and I'll help in any way I can.

Our most important focus should be on improving Isabella's word-identification skills. Because she already has relatively strong phonics skills, we need to work on increasing the amount of words she can recognize and immediately identify just by looking at them. This is called her 'sight vocabulary' (also called 'sight word vocabulary'). It would be awesome if you could work on a few specific 'sight word' strategies with Isabella this summer. Like I'd said at the IEP meeting earlier this month, it's great that she qualified for special ed help in reading at such a young age; we have time to help her catch up...but we need to work at this consistently and effectively to make it happen. It's too bad she qualified for special ed help with only two weeks left in the school year, but at least going forward she'll be getting extra help.

So, here's what I'd suggest you do. I recall that you said you read to her every day (or night), and that's wonderful. As I mentioned on the phone, there's a way to make extra-effective use of that time...just by using one simple strategy while you're reading to her.

When you read her bedtime stories, don't use the 'extra' strategy...keep doing what you're doing. Let her relax and enjoy listening to the stories. It's great to read to her like that...it helps her develop a love for literature, and that's very important. But that isn't enough, and many people miss out on utilizing a great opportunity to help their children become better readers.

So, for this 'extra' strategy...I'd suggest you use it during the day, when you do summertime reading *lessons* with her. This will be more like 'work time', when we'll be asking Isabella to work on improving her reading skills. Simply stated...have her sit at a desk or table, so she can have the book right in front of her as you read. You yourself should sit off to the side of her, and read out loud from an angle. While you (slowly) read, she needs to be pointing at, and looking at, *every* word as you read it out loud. Her job will be sliding her finger along the page, keeping her finger under each word you read. This technique will really help her improve her sight vocabulary.

Let's explore this strategy for a moment. If you're, say, sitting across from her, reading out loud, but she can't see the words you're reading (like at bedtime), she'll be improving her *listening* skills, and learning to enjoy stories…to enjoy literature. But when you read to her in that fashion, she's not learning to recognize *any* new words…not improving her sight vocabulary at all. So, during 'day lessons', as you read out loud to her, make sure the book is in front of her, and make sure she's looking at, and keeping her finger under, each word on the page as you read. Go nice and slow, but be strict about requiring her to stay with you. You'll be able to tell if she's losing focus, because she won't be pointing at the correct word…so you'll have an on-going physical indication that she's keeping her focus (or not).

Children's books tend to repeat words over and over, so she'll see them again and again as you read…and she'll begin to recognize them. And soon, she'll begin to start recognizing many words before you even say them…and that's our goal!

Isabella is already used to this technique; it's what I've used with her (and the other kids) in our pull-out reading group, so she's had a couple of weeks of experience with it. I make a big deal out of the rule. I start by saying 'okay, finger under the first word and follow along with your finger and eyeballs as I read'. I'm very strict with the policy; and kids can earn rewards if they stay with me by pointing to every word as I read.

Next fall, when her fluency improves, the 'following with finger and eyeballs' rule will stay the same, but she will get to do more and more of the reading out loud on her own…she and the other kids will share turns reading out loud. But the strict rule will be: when someone else is reading out loud, whether it's an adult or another student, it's her job to follow along with her finger and eyes. And when she's the one reading out loud, she still needs to keep her pointer finger under each word as she reads.

Side note: this will be a strategy she'll also be able to use in her mainstream classroom for years to come, as she and her classmates are all reading together during lessons in science, social studies, etc. She'll follow along with her finger while other kids have their turns to read, and of course also when she herself reads. And there's an important side benefit to this strategy: when her teacher stops the reading and asks questions or starts a discussion about what's being read, Isabella will leave her finger right on the page…right at the end of the sentence where they left off. That way, a few minutes later when the class resumes reading, she'll know right where to look on the page to start back up. We'll even teach her to use her other hand if she chooses to raise her hand to answer questions, so that she can keep her place even when she's involved in the discussion.

So, that's the strategy I'd suggest you use this summer. You can begin to make a game out of it…a contest, or challenge. After a few weeks of lessons, tell her that now you want her to try to call out any word that she's pointing to before you say it out loud. Let her slide her finger to the next word but hesitate a second to let her say it first…especially if it's a word that you know she's able to read on her own. Maybe there could even be a reward of some kind when she says words before you do. You might want to even start keeping track of words she starts calling out. Then, you can eventually start picking out certain short sentences that you know she can mostly read on her own…to start building that fun, exciting, sense of accomplishment for her. That's what we'll continue to do in the fall.

By the way, we'll also continue working on word-attack skills here at school, so she'll get even better at sounding out words that she doesn't recognize. But for lessons at home, for now anyway, let's stick with improving her sight vocabulary.

You can make a big difference by having her work every day (or most days) at this over the summer. Even though you'll need to be strict about her 'finger-pointing' responsibility, at the same time I suggest you keep it light and fun. Start with her favorite books, and make sure you always announce reading time as a fun, exciting event. It will take work on her part, but we want it to be fun work, and we want to have her develop a strong love for reading. I once had a college professor tell the class ... we don't want to just produce kids who *can* read, we want to produce kids who *do* read. I totally agree with that.

By the way, for these 'daytime lessons', make sure you're reading books with her that are at her 'instructional' level, which is a level that's just a little harder than what she can read independently. I've attached a list of books that are at her instructional level ... several suggested titles that you'll definitely be able to find at the local library.

Let me know if you have any questions, or how I might be of any further help. All the best to you and yours ... and have a great summer!

Mr. L

THE BEST
TEACHER EVER

We can (hopefully) all look back on our school days and remember teachers who had a positive impact on our lives. I can recall many such teachers, but there was one in particular from my high school years who had a profoundly positive and inspiring impact on mine.

I grew up in a small town in western Connecticut. As the youngest of five, I got to hear lots of stories about high school as I was growing up. My siblings would tell me what it was like to be on the sports teams, or to go to school dances ... or how the classes and the homework would be so much harder than what I'd been used to in junior high. They'd also tell me which teachers to try to avoid, and which ones I might really like.

My sister Sue told me I would totally enjoy having classes with Mr. B, as he was called (and since he preferred to avoid anything resembling 'the limelight', I'll respect his preference by not using his surname). Tom was the French teacher at our high school, and sister Sue was right ... I loved having him as a teacher. I also loved having him as a close friend, as it turned out.

You can tell when teachers truly care about kids as people ... as human beings. They don't just see their work as a job; to them, it's a passion…like artists see their art, or poets their poems. You knew that Tom cared about you; not just about you doing well in his class, though he certainly did care about that. But he also cared that you did well in life…that you did as well as you possibly could in life.

He had grown up in France, so one of the great things he could offer teenagers from a little rural town was a world view about life. Teaching us a foreign language was one way he accomplished that. But he found other ways to broaden our perspectives and life-experiences, as well. For example, while other teachers took us on some memorable and educational field trips, like to our state capitol, Tom took us to visit the United Nations in New York City. It was one of many ways he inspired us to think about the world, and our places in it.

Mr. B would often have a group of us come to his classroom during our study hall time. We would get passes to his room under the pretense of needing to do extra French work, but we went there because we wanted to be around him. There was just something about Tom's personality that made us feel right at home when we were with him. He had the unique ability to be our friend while also insisting on 100% effort from us at all times. And we always did work hard for him; not because we felt we had to…but because we wanted to, because he inspired us to. I would later come to realize that his influence on me in that regard would extend far beyond the walls of his classroom.

By my senior year, Tom had already cemented himself as my favorite teacher ever. I'd had a lot of great teachers over the years, but Mr. B was in a league of his own in my mind. But despite my deep respect and affection for him, I'm sure I figured (at the time) that while I would always look back on him with great fondness, I'd most likely never see him again once I graduated. I certainly didn't suspect we'd become lifelong friends.

Then one day, sometime in the last week of my senior year, he and I were in his classroom talking about the plans we had each made for the summer break. Tom mentioned that his 'to do' list suddenly had a new item on it; apparently, a car had veered slightly off the road and knocked over his freestanding mailbox the previous evening, snapping the wooden post a few feet above ground level. He said he had made a temporary fix using the damaged post, but that he would need to hire someone fairly soon to dig up the old concrete, and install a new post. I told him that I would be happy to do that work for him, but that I wouldn't accept money for the job (other than reimbursement for a bag of Sakrete and a new four by four post). I told him I *would*, however, accept some slices of pizza when the work was done.

A few days after the school year ended, I went to his home and did that work for him. Afterwards, we sat and ate pizza and talked for a couple of hours. It was our first time socializing outside of the school, and we discovered that we had several things in common. It was a very enjoyable conversation, and prompted us to agree to keep in touch in the months and years ahead as we parted ways.

I think it's fair to say that generally when people agree to 'keep in touch', it's often a well-intended yet rhetorical agreement with little or no follow-through. It was different with Tom and me. He left town for the rest of the summer a few days after that mailbox/pizza day, but he sent me a follow-up letter to again say 'thank you' for doing that work for him. He also told me how much he enjoyed our conversation, and once again wished me the best for my upcoming first year of college. I, in turn, sent him a letter saying he was welcome, and that I wanted him to know how much I appreciated and respected all that he had done for me in high school. We actually became pretty consistent pen pals (this was in the 1970's, way before emailing was available; so, snail mail and phone calls were the only ways to keep in touch, and we did plenty of both).

Tom spent his summers up on Cape Cod, where he had a house near Hyannis Port. The following summer, when we were both on our respective summer breaks, he invited me up to visit him for a weekend.

But he insisted that I first get my mother's permission…he was sort of old-fashioned when it came to such things. My mom already had huge respect and appreciation for Tom, so she gave her blessing for the visit right away. (Side note: when my sister Sue had been in his class, Tom had taken her and her French classmates to Europe for two weeks, a trip that was unfortunately axed from the school's budget by the time I got to high school. But that trip was one of many reasons my mother had so much trust and respect for Tom).

There was another former student of his visiting him at the Cape that weekend, too. He was older than me, but I recognized him and vaguely knew who he was. As I got to know him, I noted that he and Tom had remarkably similar traits…they were both gentle-souled, kind people. I remember feeling happy and fortunate to be spending time with both of them, and appreciated the opportunity to begin to see even more of the 'non-teacher' side of Tom.

Later that summer, he and I went to a Loggins and Messina concert together. It was an awesome concert (and to this day whenever I hear the song "Vahevala", I think of Tom and that fun summer evening). Anyway, it occurred to me that night that he and I no longer had a 'teacher/former student' relationship…we were instead beginning to become good friends. And our friendship grew much stronger as the years and decades went by.

He loved reading, and he loved poetry. Tom was especially fond of Guy de Maupassant's short stories, and of Jacques Prévert's poetry. He gave me the book *Douze Contes de Maupassant* (which I didn't really have the skills to read fluently), and inspired me to read several poems by Prévert. He also introduced me to the (English-translated) writings of Jean-Paul Sartre and Albert Camus, whose books I still enjoy re-reading occasionally. I guess he had a hand in turning me into a bit of an existentialist.

I ended up moving to the Seattle area, but Tom and I still talked and emailed regularly. Whenever I visited Connecticut, I would, of course, spend time with my family. The length of my visit would dictate how many friends I would get a chance to visit, but I always made time to get together with Tom.

Moving to Seattle was also the beginning of my teaching career. I became a special education teacher…one who loved working with kids and inspiring them to be the best students, and people, they could be. I became a teacher for many reasons, but certainly Mr. B's influence was a huge factor in my decision. I could think of no better footsteps to follow down my career path, and down the road of life.

Tom eventually became ill with diabetes and other health issues, and spent a few years battling to stay alive. My last visit with him at his home in Bristol was a memorable one. We spent several hours together, and did much reminiscing about the many experiences we'd shared. We didn't usually do much of that memory lane stuff, but on that visit, we did. I had no clue at the time that it would be our last visit together, but I know now that Tom did.

A couple of weeks after I returned to Washington state, Tom passed away. I was of course devastated, but I was also thankful we'd had that wonderful last visit, and that we'd done so much happy reminiscing. That visit was my one final, lasting memory of Mr. B, piled on top of decades of other heartwarming memories. I miss him very much.

THE POETRY SESSION

"Everyone, Mr. L is here for this month's poetry lesson," said Mrs. Gearhart. "And this month, he has a special guest with him."

"Hi everybody," he said. "It's great to be back to do a poetry session with you again. You all know Miss Powers, I think? She works with me in the Resource Room."

"Hi everyone," said Miss Powers, giving the students a wave.

"This month," said Mr. L, "we're going to do something a little different. I'm going to read you a poem in French, and then you're going to give me your interpretations of the poem, like we usually do. Now, let me anticipate your question...since you don't speak French, how in the world are you going to interpret the poem?

"Well, pardon me and Miss Powers for a moment, as we set up a few things. There...this desk with the tablecloth on it is now a table in a restaurant in Paris. These dishes, and the silverware and coffeepot, are part of the scene we're creating. We'll hang our coats right here on the back of our chairs...and okay, all set."

They took a seat at the table, facing one another.

"Miss Powers and I are now seated in a restaurant somewhere in Paris. We've just finished our breakfast, and now we're going to have some coffee. If you look out the window, you can see the Eiffel Tower in the distance. You can hear conversations in French, and dishes clattering...all around us in this busy Parisian restaurant.

"As you maybe can tell, we're going to act-out the poem as I read it. Actually, I'll be reciting it. You'll be able to tell what each line means, because we'll perform everything the poet describes in his famous poem. And just like we always do, remember that I'll be asking you to interpret what the poem is about. And today, I'll also ask you to talk about the feelings, the emotions, of the characters in the poem.

"This poem is written by a poet named Jacques Prévert. He was a French poet, born in the year 1900. He was famous for writing poetry, and also for being a screenwriter...which is someone who writes movies. He's known for writing sad poems and movies. Paris, in his adult years, was ravaged by World War Two, and it affected what he wrote about, and so he's famous for writing sad poems about people going through tough times, like the people in this poem. But I don't want to give away any more of the plot, so let's get to the poem.

"To help you out, we have a short list of phrases to translate for you ahead of time. The title, '*Dejeuner du Matin*' means 'Breakfast'. 'Sans me parler' means 'without talking to me' and 'sans me regarder' means 'without looking at me'. And you might know, 'café' means 'coffee'.

"Oh, one more thing you'll need to know. The woman in the poem, the one Miss Powers is playing…is the one who's actually telling the story; it's her perspective... her point of view we're hearing. Okay, so without further ado…

"*Dejeuner du Matin*, ecrit par Jacques Prévert.

"Il a mis le café dans la tasse." (After reciting that line, he picked up the coffee pot and poured imaginary coffee into his cup).

"Il a mis le lait dans la tasse de café." (He picked up the milk container and poured some milk into the coffee).

"Il a mis le sucre dans le café au lait." (Using a teaspoon, he put some sugar in the coffee).

"Avec la petite cuiller, il a tourné." (He stirred the coffee).

"Il a bu le café au lait, et il a reposé la tasse…sans me parler." (He took a sip, then put the cup back down. He did not speak to Miss Powers, though she was looking intently at him).

"Il a allumé une cigarette, il a fait des ronds avec la fumée." (He pantomimed lighting a cigarette, then blew smoke up into the air, using circled fingers to indicate that the smoke came out as smoke rings).

"Il a mis les cendres dans le cendrier." (He flicked ashes into an ash tray).

"Sans me parler, sans me regarder." (He looked around at various things, but never at Miss Powers. And he said nothing).

"Il s'est levé. Il a mis son chapeau sur sa tête." (He stood up, and put on his hat).

"Il a mis son manteau de pluie, parce qu'il pleuvait." (He put on his rain coat).

"Et il est parti, sous la pluie, sans une parole, sans me regarder." (He walked out, without ever looking at Miss Powers, though she sat watching his every move as he left).

"Et moi, j'ai pris ma tête dans ma main, et j'ai pleuré." (Miss Powers put her face in her hands, and started crying).

Mr. L waited a few moments, to let the poem and the mood sink in.

"Sorry, I need a minute," he said, pretending to cry. "Okay, first of all, thank you Miss Powers... merci beaucoup for being part of our performance today. Trés bien, magnifique! Everyone, Miss Powers has to leave, but let's give her a hand."

Everyone clapped for her.

"Thank you everybody,' she said. "And thank you Mr. L...that was fun! Have fun giving your interpretations everyone. Au revoir!"

"Au revoir, Miss Powers," he said. "Okay folks, who'd like to get us started? What happened in that restaurant in Paris that morning? Zachary?"

"The man and woman must have had a fight during breakfast, so they weren't talking to each other by the time they were finished...by the time we got to see them. Then he left, and they were still mad at each other. At least, he was still mad."

"That's a great overview, Zachary," he said. "Awesome job of getting us started. Who has another interpretation of what went on? Aubrey?"

"The man poured himself a cup of coffee, drank the coffee without looking at his wife, and without talking with her. Then he lit a cigarette, and made smoke rings, I think that's what they're called?"

"That's right."

"Then he stood up, put on his hat and coat, and he left. He didn't say anything to her, didn't even say goodbye. Then she started crying. Yeah, they had a fight, and I agree with Zachary, it was the man who was still angry."

"Excellent job, Aubrey. Trés bien! He left without even looking at her, didn't even say au revoir…didn't say goodbye.

"By the way, this poem has someone smoking a cigarette…public service announcement…don't ever smoke cigarettes, they're extremely bad for you. Some other kids might tell you that smoking is the best way to be cool…but they're totally wrong. It's way cooler, and smarter, to recognize that smoking is very unhealthy. Just tell them you don't need stupid cigarettes to be cool…you're already cool.

"Okay, so anyway, who else would like to give their interpretation of what was going on that morning? Raigan?"

"I think they weren't husband and wife…maybe they were boyfriend and girlfriend? Maybe they just broke up, and he didn't have anything more to say to her. I think it was him that broke up with her, but she still wanted to be together with him, and that's why she cried when he left?"

"Great interpretation, Raigan! Remember, when you interpret something, you give your opinion from your point of view. So, to Raigan, they just broke up. Again, with poetry, many people can read the same poem and come away with different interpretations. Stephanie?"

"Maybe she was a stranger who happened to be sitting at the same table with him in a crowded restaurant? Maybe that's why he had nothing to say to her? Oh, wait, she probably wouldn't have cried at the end then. Never mind."

"That was a good idea though, Stephanie. But you're right, the crying at the end probably wouldn't have happened. But see, it's okay to start with an idea when making an interpretation, and then make adjustments as you think it through. Kind of like forming a hypothesis in science, and then making adjustments as you learn more. Jaxson?"

"I think it was a husband and wife, and that she had done something to hurt his feelings. I think she wanted to talk about things, but he didn't want to talk because he was still too mad at her to talk about anything?"

"That's a great interpretation, Jaxson. We don't know, we won't ever know what the reason actually was behind their lack of communication … why, and if, he was mad at her. But again, that's where interpretations are so cool. Jennifer?"

"I don't think he was mad at her … maybe she wasn't even there? Maybe she had died, and that was her ghost sitting there with him in the restaurant. He didn't speak with her or look at her because he didn't know she was sitting there with him. She was just spending time with him, just hanging out with him, because she missed him so much. And she cried at the end because she couldn't be with him anymore. Ever."

Wow. That response almost brought tears to his eyes. "Jennifer, that is an amazing interpretation! I've read this poem a thousand times and never once thought of that possibility. That is such a beautiful thought … a very unique and interesting interpretation. Good for you for thinking of that. Trés, trés bien!"

The poetry session ended a few minutes later, and Mr. L thanked everyone, then gathered up the restaurant props and left. As he walked down the hallway, he kept thinking about Jennifer's response. Leading poetry sessions often made him think of Tom, and reciting the Jacques Prévert poem in French just now of course made him think of him. But somehow, Jennifer's unique interpretation seemed to him like something Tom would have come up with. He smiled, and felt Mr. B's presence; he wanted to think that perhaps at that very moment, Tom was spending time with him, just hanging out with him, because he missed him so much.

ABOUT THE AUTHOR

Dan Lauretano has over twenty-eight years of experience in the special education field working with children and adults. He has worked as a tutor in an institution, a vocational instructor at a high school, a life-skills coach at an Association for Retarded Citizens (as such organizations were called at the time he worked there), and for two and a half decades as a special education teacher in elementary and middle schools. His breadth of experience (working with students as young as age five and adults into their sixties) gives him a valuable perspective of the lifelong challenges these individuals, and their families, face on an ongoing basis.

Dan grew up in a small town in western Connecticut. He is now retired, and lives in the South Puget Sound region of Washington State with his wife, Patty.

CPSIA information can be obtained
at www.ICGtesting.com
Printed in the USA
FSHW011958150721
83292FS

9 781950 794553